The Marblehead Lighthouse: Lake Erie's Eternal Flame

The Marblehead Lighthouse

Lake Erie's Eternal Flame

Betty Neidecker

FIRST EDITION

10 9 8 7 6 5 4 3 2 1

Cover Photograph: John Kozak
Editor: Rose Kernan
Compositor: Inkwell Publishing Services
Title Page Art: Jane Roberts
Back Cover Photo: Mae Bemis

ISBN 0-9649679-0-1

LIBRARY OF CONGRESS CATALOG CARD NUMBER: 95-076125

Contents

Preface

Probably no site in Ohio has been photographed or painted by artists more than the Marblehead Lighthouse. Yet, little has been written about it: the names and lives of the hard-working and often heroic keepers have been all but lost between the pages of history. Since 1822 sailors have counted on the Marblehead Light to help them avoid dangerous obstacles, determine their positions, and guide their ships on the shallowest, the meanest, and the oldest of the Great Lakes, Lake Erie. The Marblehead Lighthouse has two distinctions: it is the oldest lighthouse in continuous service on the Great Lakes, and the second keeper, Rachel Wolcott, was the first female keeper on the Great Lakes. This book is an attempt to tell the story of the lighthouse and its keepers and their families. A number of years ago Marie Wonnell, writer and well-known local historian, and I talked about writing a book about the Marblehead Lighthouse. Before we got around to the task, Marie passed away. Had she lived, she would have been the co-author of this book.

I want to thank the many people who provided me with the help needed in putting this book together. Their generosity and graciousness have been greatly appreciated and I am profoundly grateful. My good friends, Wallace and Diane Pretzer, did a thorough editing job and also made many suggestions. Mills Brandes provided some excellent pictures and personal recollections. Grace Luebke of the Elmore Public Library and Natalie Bredbeck of the Ottawa County Genealogical Society and the Ida Rupp Public Library, Port Clinton, filled in gaps about the keepers. The cover photograph of the lighthouse was made by John Kozak and the Keeper's house photograph was made by Patricia Williamsen. Karin Messner suggested the name for the book. Steve Charter of the Center for Archival Collections and Robert Graham of the Institute for Great Lakes Research, found information and pictures. Likewise, Thomas Baker of the Marblehead Coast Guard Station provided sources for material. Early lighthouse pictures were provided by Peggy Bechtol of the Great Lakes Historical Society and Neil and Rosemary Merckens of Marblehead. Carol Poh Miller, a historical consultant in Cleveland, made available records on the Marblehead Light from her research at the National Archives in Washington, D.C. Valuable information on publishing and marketing books was generously shared by Linda Brown and Anna Bovia. Rose Kernan, my editor at Inkwell, has been patient and immeasurably helpful throughout this entire process.

Interviews and correspondence with the following persons yielded much valuable information: author, Gordon Wendt who is knowledgeable about the marine history of Sandusky Bay; Ethel Wilbur who put me in touch with a descendant of one of the lighthouse keepers; Jane Roberts who lent her artistic abilities: Luther and Thelma Marquart who searched for information about Rachel Wolcott; Mark and Julanne Owings who found the poem, "Erie"; Coast Guard Auxiliary officer, Robert Reiger, and Marblehead Mayor, Kay Dziak, provided information about visitors and lighthouse weddings; the lighthouse brides, Janett St. Clair, Janice Gstalder, Janet Fallat and Ethel Inman, shared stories of their weddings at the lighthouse. In 1981, I taped an interview with the late Hilda Kelly Nelson, a descendant of Benajah Wolcott; she told of the wedding of Benajah's granddaughter, Eliza, and John Kelly, at the Wolcott home on Bayshore Road.

Much information was gleaned from genealogical records. Marian Stephens, a descendant of Benajah Wolcott, shared her research of the family. I also relied heavily on the genealogical records compiled by my father, the late Fred Neidecker.

Erie

by Berton Braley
(ca. 1915)

She's shallow and muddy and mean,
She's chuck full of sandbars and such,
She's pretty when calm and serene,
But she's never that way very much.
You hardly can sail by the chart,
Her shoals keep a-shiftin' around,
You'll think that you know her by heart,
When - crunch - and your boat is aground!

She's blowsy an' bleary
An' nasty - is Erie,
An' always just ripe for a squall,
She makes us all weary
An' ugly, does Erie,
The meanest old lake of them all.

Superior's icy and rough.
An' Huron is ugly at times;
Old Michigan's frequently tough,
But for faults, misdemeanors an' crimes,
Old Erie - out there in the east -
Has got them all distanced in style.
She's a most undependable beast
With a temper that's certainly vile.

You want to be leery
An' careful of Erie;
She's husky, although she is small -
A pugnacious dearie -
A fighter is Erie -
The meanest old lake of them all!

She's choppy an' fickle an' slick:
One minute she's sweet as a dream,
The next - she'll be makin' you sick
An' standing the ship on her beam.
The wind-jammers hates her like sin,
The steamers is fond of her - not -
She's ought to be pinched an' run in,
She's the wickedest one of the lot.

So don't get too cheery
Or flip with Lake Erie,
She's primed for a bluff or a brawl,
For sailin' is skeery
An' risky on Erie,
The meanest old lake of them all!

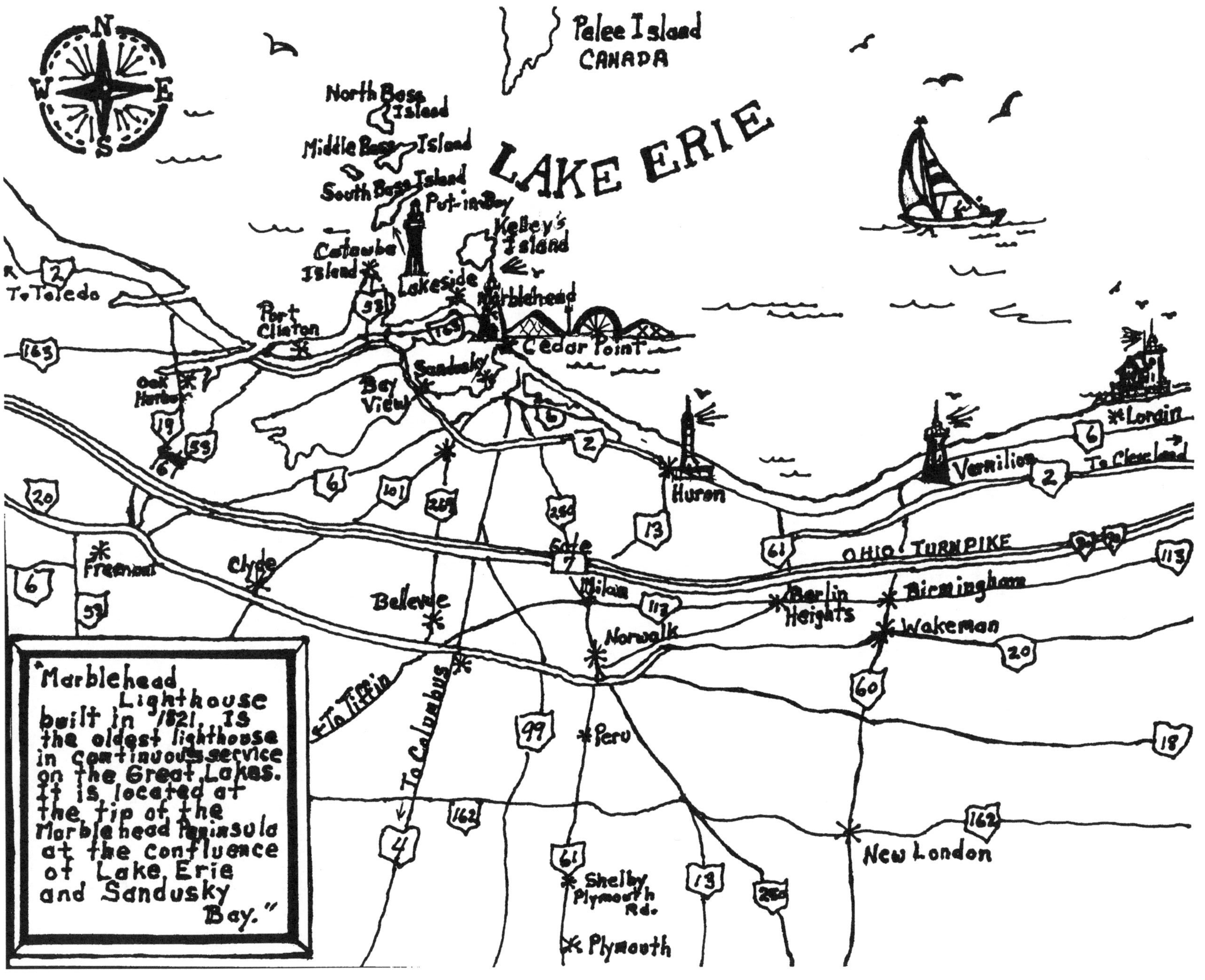

N
E
S
W
Pelee Island
CANADA
LAKE ERIE
North Bass Island
Middle Bass Island
South Bass Island
Put-in-Bay
Catawba Island
Lakeside
Kelley's Island
Marblehead
Cedar Point
Port Clinton
To Toledo
Oak Harbor
Bay View
Sandusky
Huron
Vermilion
Lorain
To Cleveland
OHIO TURNPIKE
Gate 7
Fremont
Clyde
Bellevue
Milan
Norwalk
Berlin Heights
Birmingham
Wakeman
To Tiffin
To Columbus
Peru
New London
Shelby Plymouth Rd.
Plymouth
2
163
19
53
6
20
101
269
250
13
61
113
60
18
99
162
4
"Marblehead Lighthouse built in 1821, IS the oldest lighthouse in continuous service on the Great Lakes. It is located at the tip of the Marblehead Peninsula at the confluence of Lake Erie and Sandusky Bay."

1

Lake Erie Gets a Lighthouse

At the edge of the village of Marblehead, Ohio, on the shore of Lake Erie a sign proclaims that this is the location of the Marblehead Lighthouse, built in 1821. It is the oldest lighthouse in continuous service on the Great Lakes. State Route 163, which is Main Street, winds through the town, passing small homes built close to the road, Biro's Factory which makes meat cutting tools, the Neuman and Kelley Island Ferry Lines, the Galley Restaurant, an ice cream stand, the Marblehead Bank, the VFW, and Mutach's Grocery. Just off Main Street is the United States Coast Guard Station. One of the busiest stations on the Great Lakes, the Marblehead Station, first known as the Marblehead Lifesaving Station, was established in 1876.

Gift and clothing shops with names suggesting the other Marblehead in Massachusetts, the Richmond Art Gallery, as well as the *Peninsula News* office, Kukay's Restaurant, the Marathon Oil station, the True Value

Hardware store, a cluster of gift shops, and a notion store which seems to have everything "from calico to codfish" line the street. A little farther down is the Schoolhouse Gallery, a restored schoolhouse selling gifts, antiques, art, and ice cream. Holy Assumption Orthodox Church, with its beautiful interior, is across the street from a cemetery. Further down are motels, cottages for rent, bait stores, and a boat basin.

State Route 163 follows Lake Erie closely because the entire center of the Marblehead Peninsula is a huge limestone quarry which has employed Marblehead residents for several generations. Lake freighters, tied up within sight of Main Street, carry the stone to varied places. For example, limestone was used to build the locks at Sault Ste. Marie and, closer to home, it was used in the 1840s to build locks on the Miami and Erie Canal at what is now Sidecut Park in Maumee. Quarry workers who came from "the old country" first lived in a huge barn-like structure still standing on Main Street. Alexander Clemons, who moved to Marblehead from Kelleys Island in 1834, operated the first quarry; his home is, at present, operated as a bed and breakfast inn on Clemons Street.

Main Street continues "around the horn" of the Marblehead Peninsula. Next to beautiful St. Mary Byzantine Catholic Church with its onion-shaped spires, a small lane leads to the Marblehead Lighthouse standing on the west bank of Sandusky Bay where it joins Lake Erie. Since it was built in 1821, it has been guiding mariners without interruption. Originally called the "Sandusky Bay Light," the Marblehead Lighthouse took on its present name in 1870. About ten miles from the Canadian border, this aged sentinel stands at one of the stormiest spots on Lake Erie—the oldest, the shallowest, the most treacherous, and the most unpredictable of the Great Lakes. Adding to the grandeur of this venerable sentinel are huge slabs of

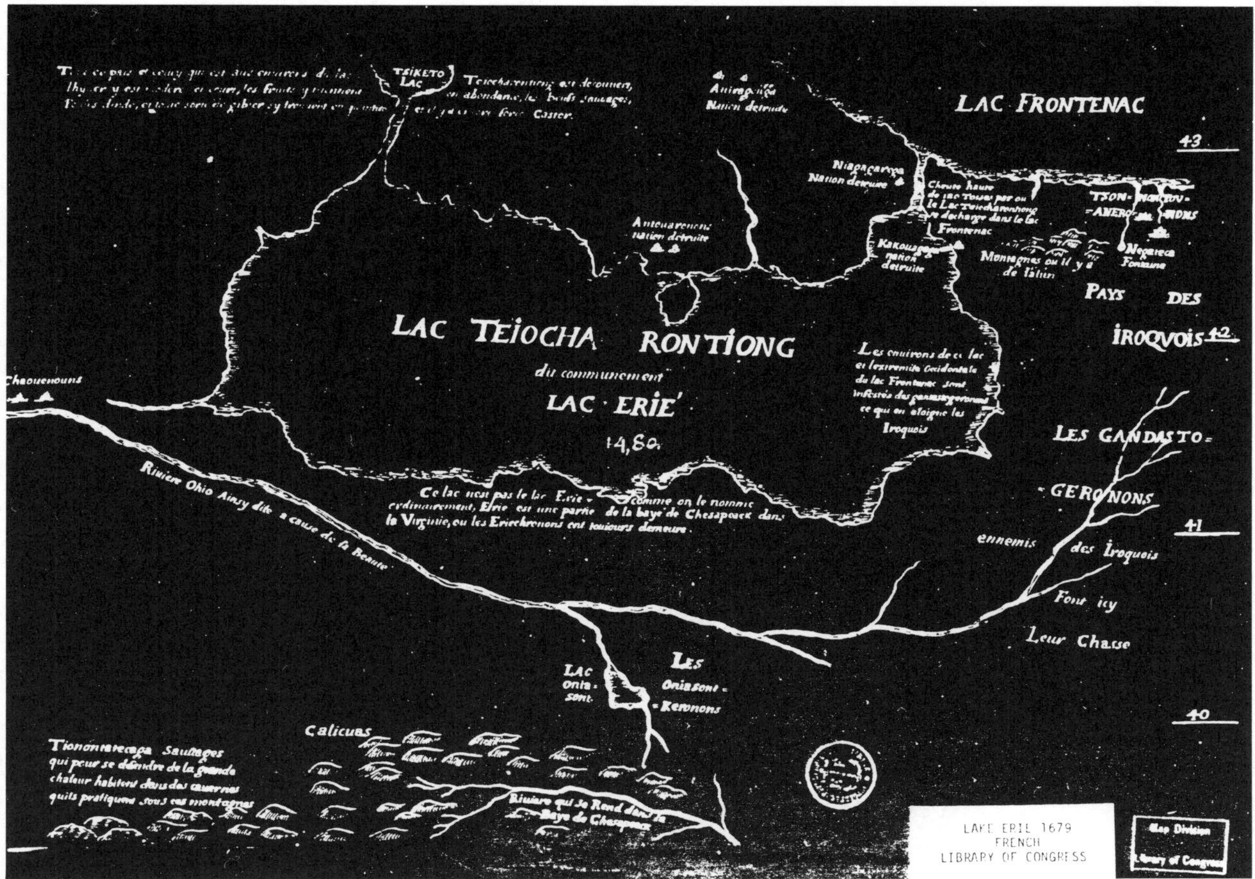

Figure 1-1. *The French explorers map of the area surrounding Lake Erie in 1679.* Courtesy of the Library of Congress, Geography and Map Division, Washington D.C.

limestone, trees gnarled by wind and water, and an eerie solitude; artists and photographers frequently capture this exquisite grandeur. Except for the addition of fifteen feet to its height in 1897, it looks much the same as it did in 1821.

Actually, little has been written about the Marblehead Lighthouse and only passing mention of it appears in general books about lighthouses. Its simple, structural beauty and uninterrupted service since 1822 are like the comforting presence of a faithful old friend.

From the base of the lighthouse, and across Lake Erie to the north, is Kelleys Island. Somewhat northwest, on a clear day South Bass Island and Put-In-Bay come into view. Southeast across the mouth of Sandusky Bay is Cedar Point Amusement Park, mecca of thousands of summer visitors. To the northeast is a clear sweep of water all the way to Buffalo, New York. From this direction, Lake Erie sometimes lashes out with a violent storm known to the residents of the peninsula as a "three-day nor'easter."

Lighthouses have been around for many centuries. The earliest one we know of, the Pharos Light in Alexandria, Egypt, was built in 285 B.C. This beacon lasted about 1,500 years before being toppled by an earthquake. The Phoenicians and Romans also built light towers before the birth of Christ. Following the Dark Ages, when Europeans began trading among themselves, they built lighthouses to facilitate increased shipping. Many of these used wood fires on top of stone towers. Later, after some advances in mining, coal was used as the main fuel for the lights.

One of the best-known lighthouses, the Eddystone Light, was built in England in 1698. This storm-ravaged lighthouse was first built on the rocky coast of England at Lands End. Construction was very difficult because of its location, and several times it was destroyed by fierce storms and fires that often resulted in the loss of lives. Eventually, it was taken down, piece by piece, and rebuilt at Plymouth on a firmer foundation and with a higher tower. For generations the Eddystone Light led ships to port, mariners to safety, and one mermaid to ruin as described in the well-known folk song, "The Keeper of the Eddystone Light."

There is a seventy-foot replica of the Eddystone Light at Grand Lake St. Mary's in West Central Ohio, located halfway between St. Mary's and Celina. It may be the only lighthouse on an inland lake in Ohio.

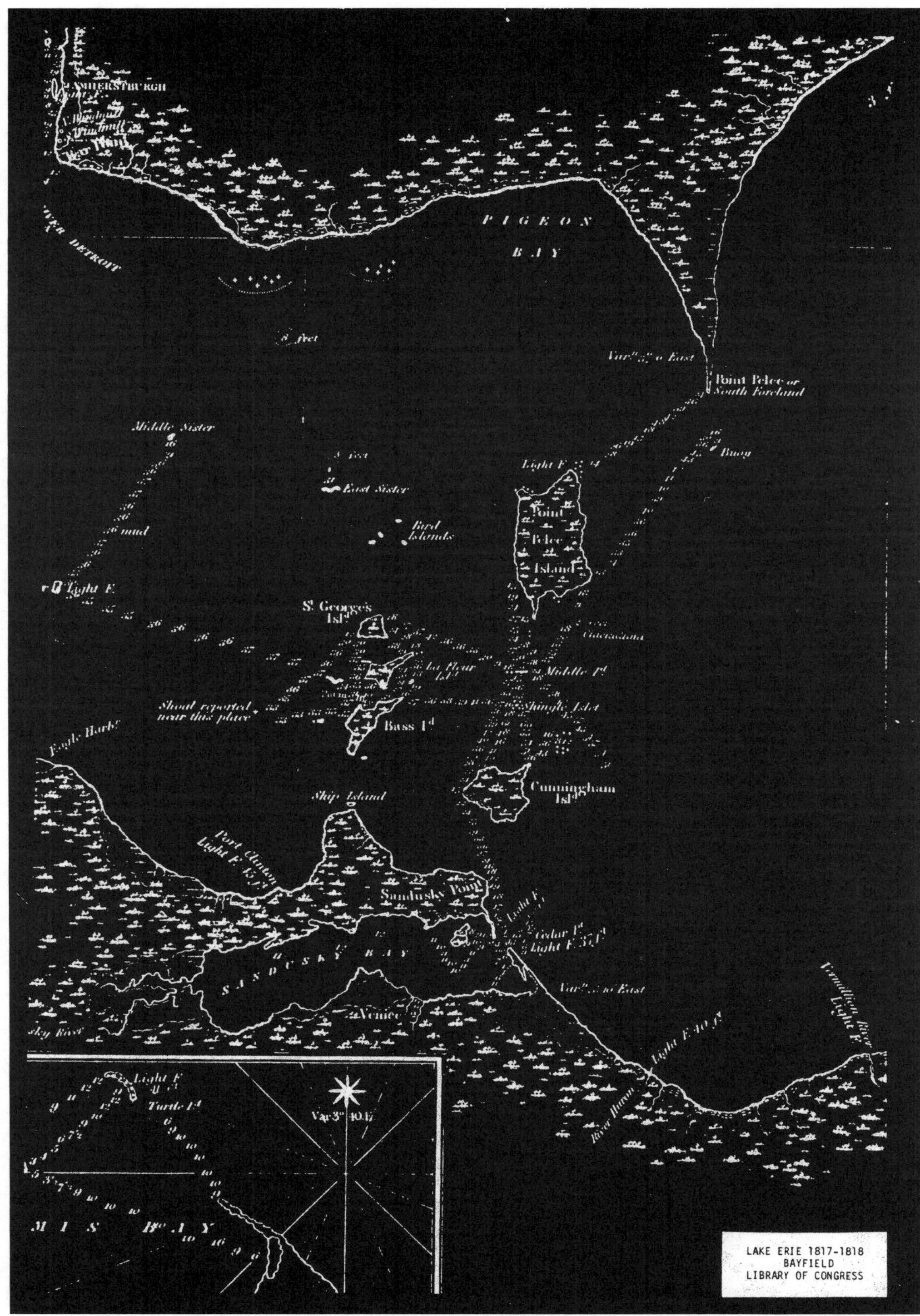

Figure 1-2. *1817–1818 map showing future lighthouse locations in the Western Basin of Lake Erie.* Courtesy of the Library of Congress, Geography and Map Division, Washington D.C.

Grand Lake was created as a reservoir for the Miami and Erie Canal in the mid-1800s. The lighthouse is on private property, but may be viewed from the road.

The first permanent lighthouse to be built in the United States was located in Boston Harbor and was built of stone in 1716. It used either candles or lamps for its light. In 1751, the wooden part of the tower was destroyed by fire and, in 1776, the British blew it up. Replaced in 1783, the Boston Harbor Light has undergone many improvements throughout the years; functioning even today and automated in 1989, it was the last staffed lighthouse in the United States.

While the Marblehead Lighthouse is the oldest in continuous service on the Great Lakes, it was not the first to be built. A lighthouse was built in Buffalo, New York in 1818. It still stands but is not used. The Old Presque Isle Light in Erie, Pennsylvania, built in 1819, was replaced in 1867 by a sandstone tower and permanently removed from service in 1897. The Charlotte-Genesee Light in Rochester, New York was built in 1822 and discontinued in 1881. In 1759, the British captured Fort Niagara from the French at the juncture of the Niagara River and Lake Ontario and, by 1780, placed a beacon on top of the fort known as the "French Castle." This served as a guiding light until 1823, when a wooden lighthouse was constructed. It was abandoned in 1872 when a light tower was completed south of the fort on the shore of Lake Ontario.

The earliest inhabitants of the southern shore of Lake Erie were Native American Indians–the Senecas, Hurons, Ottawas, Delawares, Wyandots, Miamis, Chippewas, and Eries. The Eries, known as the "Cat Nation," were the first to come into the lake region. They were nearly annihilated by the Iroquois in 1656 ; those who escaped were incorporated with other tribes. On the south shore of Kelleys Island, the famous Inscription Rock with its pictographs was

Figure 1-3. *Today, visitors may visit the Indian Inscription Rock on Kelleys Island. Since this photograph was made many years ago, the figures and symbols are barely discernible.* Author's postcard collection.

brought to the attention of the white man about 1833 and interpreted by Shingvauik, a learned Indian. The figures and symbols, now nearly obliterated by the elements but carefully preserved in the Smithsonian Institute in Washington D.C., tell the story of the occupation of the island by the Eries, the coming of the Wyandots, the final triumph of the Iroquois, and the virtual annihilation of the Eries who became the "Lost Nation" yet left their name upon the lake.

The Indian cultures in Ohio diminished in the mid -to-late seventeenth century when early French explorers and missionaries arrived. One of the first explorers was Etienne Brule, a French scout. Legend has it that he landed on All Saint's Day at the mouth of a river in what is now Ottawa County, and named it appropriately "Toussaint" or "All Saints." The French explorers left evidence of their presence in the area with such names as LaCarne, Lacarpe Creek, Portage River, Huron River, Vermillion, and Chappelle Creek. The French Canadians who settled in the region were mainly hunters, trappers, and fishermen. Today, many French family names can be found in Ottawa and Lucas Counties.

In the early 1800s, Ohio was a wilderness; the northwest area was the impenetrable Great Black Swamp. Settlement was encouraged by the United States government following the Revolutionary War. Northeastern Ohio was designated the "Connecticut Western Reserve," of which the western part was known as the "Firelands Western Reserve." Land was granted to those residents of Connecticut whose homes and towns had been burned by the British during the Revolution. Much of this land, however, was purchased from the original grantees by land speculators and developers for ridiculously low prices and sold to early settlers for inflated prices. A slow migration of families westward to Ohio, temporarily halted by the War of 1812, resulted from this speculation. After Commodore Oliver Hazard Perry defeated the British Navy on Lake Erie on September 13, 1813, the southern shore of Lake Erie again opened up to settlers.

Noting severe economic depression after the War of 1812, President James Monroe and Speaker of the House Henry Clay believed the key to the region's recovery and prosperity to be transportation. Already under construction, the Erie Canal would link the eastern seaboard to Lake Erie. By 1819, many vessels were already sailing the Great Lakes and settlers were gaining in numbers all along the lake shore. To overcome the enormous barrier caused by Niagara Falls and the Niagara River, namely a drop of 326 feet from Lake

Erie to Lake Ontario, the Canadians built the Welland Canal which successfully linked the two Lakes.

The dangers of navigating the Lakes were apparent. The first paddle steamer on the Lakes, *Walk-in-the-Water*, ran into the very teeth of stormy weather. She sailed regularly between Buffalo and Detroit, calling weekly at Cunningham's (Kelleys) Island to buy firewood. On the last day of October 1821, however, she was wrecked off Point Abino near Buffalo.

One of the most treacherous areas was the south passage through Lake Erie comprising the channel between the Bass Islands and Kelleys Island to the north and the Marblehead Peninsula and Catawba Island to the south. The narrowness of the channel, the rocky shoreline, and the sudden unpredictable storms urgently necessitated navigational aids.

Even though there were lighthouses in this nation as early as 1716, sixty years before the Declaration of Independence, Congress did not recognize their importance until 1792 when it passed the law creating the Lighthouse Establishment as a unit of the Federal Government and delegated the authority to the Secretary of the Treasury. The responsibility for lighthouses alternated for a number of years between the Secretary of the Treasury and the Commissioner of Revenue until Stephen Pleasonton, Fifth Auditor of the United States Treasury, took full responsibility. Serving from 1820 until 1852, he had no nautical background but was a zealous bookkeeper who allowed little latitude for expenditures and improvements.

Eventually recognizing the need for navigational aids on the Great Lakes, the United States Congress appropriated $5,000 on March 3, 1819 for a "lighthouse at or between the mouth of the Grand River in the State of Ohio and the mouth of the Detroit River in the Territory of Michigan." Because this amount was not considered sufficient, Congress appropriated an additional $5,000 on May 15, 1820 to complete the lighthouse. Pleasonton decided on a location 72 miles from the Grand River and ninety miles from the Detroit River; in 1821 he purchased three additional acres for $300. He also authorized the purchase of land for a lighthouse from the estate of Epaphraditus Bull, who owned the eastern end of the Marblehead Peninsula as well as Bull's Island, now known as Johnson's Island. James Stevens, the Connecticut Representative to the Sixteenth Congress, made the motion to purchase the land. As the attorney for Bull's estate, Stevens was attempting to promote the building of a city on Bull's Island. In *Sandusky's Yesterdays,* Frohman gives this account on choosing the exact location for the lighthouse:

> "James Kilbourne, one of the proprietors of Sandusky, went with U.S. Commissioner Col. Foster to fix the site for a lighthouse. He showed him Cape Sandy at the entrance to Sandusky Harbor, and Rocky Point at the end of the Marblehead Peninsula. The latter was chosen."

"Cape Sandy" was an early name for Cedar Point and "Rocky Point" was a part of Bull's estate. Eventually, Rocky Point became Point Marblehead and today we know it as Marblehead.

Given the contract for construction, Stephen Wolverton of Erie County, in turn, subcontracted to William Kelly, who, with his 13-year-old son, John Reid Kelly as a member of the crew, built the Marblehead Lighthouse of native limestone quarried nearby. William Kelly, Sandusky's first stone mason, had built many of the fine old homes in that city. He worked for $1.50 a day; his helpers, A. Hartshorn and Smith, each for 87-½ cents per day. In addition, Amos Fenn of Clyde also helped. According to *The Firelands Pioneer* (June, 1868)

Figure 1-4. *The Fresnel lens was placed in the Marblehead Lighthouse in 1897 and removed in 1972. Now exhibited at the Marblehead Coast Guard Station.* Author's photo.

"Messrs Fenn and Smith then went to the Peninsula, where they remained for some time, assisting to erect and finish off the lighthouse at Marblehead." A competent builder, Fenn, who had migrated from Litchfield, Connecticut, in 1817, had helped in the construction of several buildings in Sandusky.

Specifications called for the tower to be fifty feet above the ground, the base to be twenty-five feet in diameter, and the diameter at the top to be twelve feet.

The base wall was to be five feet thick, tapering to a thickness of two feet at the top. In addition to the money for construction, a sum of $6,520 was provided for a keeper's dwelling. In a letter to Pleasanton dated June 24, 1822, Col. Foster stated, "I returned a few days since from inspecting the Light House etc., built by Stephen Woolverton near the entrance into Sandusky Bay, Huron County, State of Ohio. I am happy to inform you that the buildings are erected agreeably to contract and completed in a masterly workmanlike manner."

The first keeper was Benajah Wolcott, who signed for the lighthouse in a letter dated June 17, 1822: "Possession of three acres of land at Rocky Point on the Shore of Lake Erie, west of the entrance into Sandusky Bay in Huron County of Ohio—with a Lighthouse, Dwelling house, Kitchen and accompany out house there on erected, finished and in complete order, with the windows glazed in each, with good well water, water bucket, chain and krib—..."

In 1870, the name was changed from "Sandusky Bay Light" to "Marblehead Lighthouse." Its exterior, untouched until 1880, was then covered with stucco and painted white. In 1897, when fifteen feet of brick construction was added to the top of the tower, its height increased to sixty-five feet. When the lighthouse was being repaired in 1969, the stucco was removed and the original stonework and brickwork could be seen. Oblong openings in the masonry, about five feet apart, made a spiral pattern all the way to the top; places where timbers were cast into the stonework supported the scaffold for the next round of timbers. In 1974, following a severe flood, water boiled around the base of the lighthouse and rocks bombarding the structure caused considerable damage. The Interior Department, concerned that further damage would cause deterioration, had a gunnite surface applied after the entire tower was skinned, repointed, and put in condition for the sealing coat.

Although lighthouses have been built in many shapes, designs, colors, materials, and thicknesses, their most important task is to support the light guiding mariners during the nighttime. During the daylight hours, the tower itself serves as a landmark (its secondary function); its primary function, however, is to provide a navigational aid. The earliest lights, namely bonfires on the shore or lanterns hung from trees along coastal areas, guided ships to safety but in some areas lured unwary sailors to rocky coasts where their ships were wrecked and the cargoes looted. Although the very earliest lighthouses used wood as fuel and some used coal, candles were another way of producing light. Oil lamps with wicks were used later, and the early lighthouse keepers were often called "wickies."

Winslow Lewis, a retired ship's captain, made the original lighting fixture in the Marblehead Lighthouse. This apparatus consisted of thirteen Argand whale oil lamps, each with a sixteen-inch reflector. The contract, however, called for fifteen patent lamps, fifteen nine-inch reflectors and nine-inch lenses. Lewis maintained that his arrangement would make a better light than the ones called for in the contract specifications. In the long run, this change proved expensive for lighthouses using Lewis' equipment.

In 1858, the Marblehead lighting fixture was refitted with a Fourth Order Fresnel lens. August Fresnel, a French physicist, had developed the lens in 1822. It resembled a glass beehive, and in the center was a single lamp; the light refracted, magnified, and produced a concentrated beam. Because whale oil and sperm oil had become scarce and costly, they were no longer used. The new lamp operated first on lard oil; beginning in 1899, kerosene was used. This was probably

Figure 1-5. *The clockwork mechanism used to rotate the light, giving it an intermittent signal. The keeper cranked the weights (housed in a large pipe) to the top and, as they descended, the metal table revolved causing the light to "flash." Now on display at the Marblehead Coast Guard Station.* Author's photo.

the incandescent oil vapor lamp, in which kerosene was forced into a vaporizer chamber where it struck hot walls and instantly changed into a vapor. In the days before electricity, which was first installed in 1923, keeping the light burning was both difficult and dangerous. The lighthouse keeper's wife and children frequently helped by climbing the spiral staircase in the tower, tending the light and cleaning the apparatus.

Figure 1-6. *Two oil houses are at the left of the lighthouse. They were needed when oil was used to fuel the lamps.* Official United States Coast Guard Photo.

In 1897, fifteen feet were added to the top of the tower, making space for a watch room. A newer and larger Fresnel lens was ordered from Paris and installed after it had been exhibited at the St. Louis World's Fair. The old lantern was replaced by one from the Erie, Pennsylvania, main light. At this time, a rotating mechanism called a "clockwork system" (because it was energized by a falling weight) was installed to rotate the light, giving it an intermittent signal. The mechanism was like a giant grandfather clock, its weights contained in a large pipe in the center of the tower. Each night, every three hours, the keeper cranked the weights up to the top and, as the weights descended, the metal table revolved causing the light to "flash." Each lighthouse had an assigned frequency; by timing the light, the mariner could identify it and determine his location.

In 1930, the United States Lighthouse Service became part of the United States Coast Guard. An automatic plastic lens replaced the old Fresnel lens in 1972. The color was changed from ruby red to a flashing green light with a 10.8 mile range and 1,087 candle power. Today, the Aids to Navigation Team located in Huron, Ohio is responsible for the operation of the Marblehead Light. The Old Fresnel lamp is now on display at the Coast Guard Station in Marblehead. After its removal from the lighthouse, it was moved to Toledo and then to the Coast Guard Station in Detroit where Marblehead residents Robert Boytim, Frank Merrill, and Jim Minier tracked it down. They decided it should be returned to Marblehead so they dismantled and carefully wrapped it, took it down from the fifth floor of the Station in Detroit, and brought it back to the Village Hall. Now on loan from Marblehead to the Coast Guard Station, it may be viewed and admired as an important part of the history of the area.

In addition to the light tower, other structures were necessary for the livelihood and well-being of the lightkeepers and their families. In his acceptance letter, Benajah Wolcott, first keeper, listed a dwelling house, kitchen, and accompanying out houses. The original dwelling was built of limestone from the surrounding area. Built in 1880, the present keeper's house (now occupied by personnel from the Ohio Department of Natural Resources) is of frame construction, one-and-a-half stories, with clapboard siding, a steeply pitched gable roof, and a small porch. The assistant keeper's apartment occupied the upstairs. Mills Brandes, who

Figure 1-7. *The second dwelling on the property, built in 1880 for the keeper and his family. The assistant keeper lived in an upstairs apartment. At the far left is a combined coal storage house and privy. The barn in the center, still standing, was built in 1896 to replace the original barn.* Official United States Coast Guard photo.

lived at the lighthouse in the 1920s with his grandparents, Captain and Mrs. Charles Hunter, remembers a well and a huge tree between the lighthouse and the keeper's house. The well was not used at that time, but he recalls a cistern in the basement.

Before electricity, fuel for the light was usually stored at the keeper's house but when highly flammable kerosene and mineral oil supplanted sperm and lard oil, Congress (in 1888) authorized detached oil storage houses. Old photographs and postcards of the lighthouse grounds show two such oil houses. The

Figure 1-8*. The combined privy and coal storage building was moved several times in the area and today is on private property and used as a guest house.* Author's photo.

first one to be built, a circular iron structure lined with brick and fitted with iron shelves, had a capacity of 225 gallons of oil. The next iron oil house, built in 1906, was square, red, brick-lined, and fitted with iron shelves. With a capacity of 600 gallons, it was located twenty-one feet southwest of the light tower. With electrification of the lights in 1920, the purpose for fuel storage buildings no longer existed.

One of the earliest buildings still standing on the grounds of the lighthouse is the barn, which was necessary for the keeper's and his family's animals, equipment, and supplies. To maintain their daily liv-

Figure 1-9. *An addition was made to the barn when an icehouse was moved and attached and later used as a carriage house.* Author's photo.

ing, they had horses and cattle and had to raise most of their own fruits, vegetables, and grains. The age of this barn has not been specifically determined, but legend has it that the third keeper of the lighthouse, Jeremiah Van Benschoten (1834-1841) and husband of Benajah Wolcott's widow, had a barn in which he kept wild Indian ponies. Appearing to be in good condition, the barn is a combination of clapboard, board and batten, and wood shingle siding with a shed-roofed addition. An icehouse was moved and attached to the barn and was later used as a carriage house. A boat house was also on the grounds, as well as a cement walk from the tower to the oil house, well, and dwelling, and from the dwelling to the fuel house and barn.

Another building, formerly on the grounds of the lighthouse, is a twelve by sixteen-foot wooden building which was a combined coal storage house and privy. Now on private property, not far from the lighthouse, it belongs to Ron and Deb Miller who converted it into an attractive guest house.

In the 1960s, the lighthouse and the keeper's house almost suffered fatal blows. Local residents voiced their anger when they heard that the light would be demolished and replaced with a metal skeleton atop which a transistorized light would be affixed. There were also plans to raze the 1880s keeper's house. R. Neil Merckens, a great-great-great grandson of Benajah Wolcott and President of the Ottawa County Historical Society, intervened; with the help of members of the Society and U.S. Congressman Delbert Latta, the house escaped demolition. The Historical Society attempted to buy the house to use as a museum, but it was turned over to the Department of Natural Resources and today is used as housing for its employees.

Reprinted at the end of this chapter is a copy of a clipping file of brief annual reports on the property for the years between 1837 and 1906 (National Archives, Washington D.C.). The report confirms the fact that a keeper's dwelling was built on lighthouse grounds when it (the lighthouse) was built in 1821. Not only are there references to the keeper's dwelling but comments are made about other buildings. Some of the reports, however, are puzzling; for example, information from the Treasury Department, Fifth Auditor's Office, May 13, 1842, cites expenses at the time of the building of the lighthouse. The next comment states, "No part of this statement is true."

Interesting to note are the references to the bad condition of the keeper's dwelling, beginning in 1868,

Figure 1-10. *Probably the earliest photograph of the Marblehead Lighthouse. Built of native limestone, the tower's base is 25 feet in diameter and the walls are five feet thick. In 1897, fifteen feet were added to the tower.* Photographer unknown. Courtesy of Neil and Rosemary Merckens.

when repair of the plastering was authorized and continued for the next thirteen years. Finally, in 1882 "the old stone dwelling was taken down; the grounds around the new dwelling were graded and covered with loam" and the light tower underwent extensive repairs and is still standing today.

There are eighty-seven steps to the top of the Lighthouse. On certain specified Saturdays during the summer and fall months, hundreds of visitors climb to the top to admire the view. The Marblehead Peninsula Chamber of Commerce and the U.S. Coast Guard Auxillary coordinate the popular tours, which started on June 26, 1986. At any time of the year, visitors come to the Lighthouse to sketch or paint, to take photographs, to walk on the rough shoreline, and to enjoy the picnic grounds. The Marblehead Lighthouse is on the National Register of Historic Places.

Report of Lieut, G. J. Pendergrast, U.S.N., to the President of the Board of Navy Commissioners. Erie, Pa., August 18, 1837.

X X X X X

Sandusky light-house.—This is a highly important light, in consequence of its showing the entrance to Sandusky bay, and also as serving as a director through the island passage. There was a beacon-light authorized to be placed as a guide into this harbor; and I have recommended, in my report on the subject, that it be made a red light, so as to distinguish it from Sandusky light-house, and have selected Cedar point as the site for it. Four miles north of Sandusky light-house is Cunningham Island.

Report of Lieut. C.T. Platt, U.S.N., to the Secretary of Treasury. Geneva, N.Y., November 26, 1838.

X X X X X

Sandusky light-house has fifteen lamps, and thirteen lighted with thirteen bright reflectors; all in good order and fixed. The light is in commendable order, and the materials furnished by the contractor are faultless. This light-house is an important one, from its favorable location, in making the spacious bay of Sandusky.

Treasury Department, Fifth Auditor's Office, May 13, 1842.

X X X X X

1847

"Sandusky light-house, erected in 1821, at a cost of $4,250; expenses on foundation in 1822, $2,520; rebuilt, owing to its dilapidation and decay, 1838, at a cost of $3,000."

No part of this statement is true. The light-house was erected at a cost of $7,232; the $2,520 mentioned above being part of that sum. Nothing was ever paid for recurring the foundation, nor was it ever rebuilt at all. The light-house now stands in good condition as it was built, 21 years ago.

1854

At Sandusky light-house, copper ventilators were placed in the base of the lantern.

1858

"Important repairs have been made at Presque Isle, Grand River, *Sandusky,* and Grassy Island light-houses, and other repairs of lesser importance have been made to various light-houses on Lake Ontario."

1868

37. *Sandusky.*—Repair of plastering of keeper's dwelling has been authorized; a store-room for wicks, chimneys, paints and oils, is required. These articles are now kept in the kitchen.

1869 44. *Sandusky.*—This station is in good condition. A boat-house will be built this season.

1877 559. *Marblehead, Sandusky Bay, Lake Erie, Ohio.*—This station is in bad condition. The house is old, leaky, and barely habitable. It should be rebuilt. This is one of the most important lights on Lake Erie; all vessels passing through the lake to the southward of the islands must make it, and it must always be kept up. The tower is also in bad condition. The estimated cost of rebuilding the station is $20,000, and an appropriation of that amount is recommended.

1878 560. *Marblehead, Sandusky Bay, Lake Erie, Ohio.*—The dwelling and outer wall of the tower are in bad condition. The house is not habitable in cold weather and is unfit for use as a dwelling at any time. A small frame shed of one room was put up last year, and this the keeper and his family occupy during cold weather. The new dwelling and tower recommended by the board in its last annual report are urgently needed. This is one of the most important stations on the lakes, as the channel between it and the islands is the thoroughfare for all vessels passing up and down the lake, except those running directly between Eastern ports and the Detroit River. An appropriation of $20,000 is required to put the station in proper order.

1879 587. *Marblehead, Sandusky Bay, Lake Erie, Ohio.*—Last year's recommendation in respect to this station is renewed. The keeper's dwelling is not inhabitable, and should be rebuilt, as should the tower. This work, it is estimated, will cost $20,000. An appropriation of that amount is accordingly suggested.

1880 597. *Marblehead, Sandusky Bay, Lake Erie, Ohio.*—Some repairs were made to the out-buildings at this station. The dwelling being past repair, it will be rebuilt this season. The tower must be rebuilt at an estimated cost of $11,000.

1881 607. *Marblehead, on the northeast end of Marblehead, and south side of entrance to the channel between Kelly and Bass Islands and the mainland, Lake Erie, Ohio.*—The keeper's dwelling was entirely rebuilt. The wood-house was altered to a summer kitchen and was moved to a more suitable locality. Some minor repairs were made. A boat-landing is needed, which will cost $800. The tower is old and dilapidated; it should be replaced by a new one, which will cost about $11,000.

1882 612. *Marblehead, on the northeast end of Marblehead, Ohio.*—The old stone dwelling was taken down; the grounds around the new dwelling were graded and covered with loam. The tower and dwelling received various minor repairs. A new tower should be built at this station to replace the old stone structure now in use, which will soon require extensive repairs to render it serviceable.

1886 752. *Marblehead, Lake Erie, Ohio.*—A veranda was built in front of the kitchen, the walk leading from the dwelling to the barn and boat-house was rebuilt, the boat-house was moved 150 feet to the southward, and enlarged, and new boat ways were built and bolted to the rock face. The board fence inclosing the site and right of way was replaced by a wire fence with iron posts placed on the line of the recent survey, and minor repairs were made.

1891 1115. *Marblehead, on northeast end of Marblehead, Lake Erie, Ohio.*—The metalwork for a circular oil house, which was procured by contract, was taken by the tender from Cleveland, Ohio, and delivered at the station, together with the cement for the foundation and brick lining. The metalwork was put together at the station and placed upon a concrete foundation, prepared upon a rock surface, and it was lined with brick. The oil house was located in the rear of the tower and between it and the dwelling.

1898 1263. *Marblehead, west of entrance to Sandusky Bay, Lake Erie, Ohio.*—The old stone masonry of the upper 8 feet of the tower was replaced with a vertical brick wall inclosing a watch room, furnished with closets and a cleaning shelf. Iron stairs from the watch room to the lantern, four windows in the tower and two in the watch room were provided. Repairs were made.

1901 115. *Marblehead, west of entrance to Sandusky Bay, Lake Erie, Ohio.*—The fourth-order lantern was replaced with the third-order lantern taken from the discontinued main light-tower at Erie, Pa., to increase the power of the light. Some 43 loads of cinders were placed on the driveway leading to the public highway for its improvement. Minor repairs were made.

1903 118. *Marblehead, northward and westward of entrance to Sandusky Bay, Lake Erie, Ohio.*—The fourth-order lens here was taken out and a third-order lens with clockwork revolving apparatus was installed and adjusted to produce a white flash at intervals of 10 seconds on the opening of navigation, 1903. Some 1,900 running feet of wire fence were built on the boundary lines of the light-house lot. Various repairs were made.

1905 118. *Marblehead, west of entrance to Sandusky Bay, Lake Erie, Ohio.*—The metal work for a square iron oilhouse was purchased.

1906 115. *Marblehead, west of entrance to Sandusky Bay, Lake Erie, Ohio.*—An iron oilhouse, with a capacity of 540 gallons, was built. A concrete walk was laid from the oil house to the walk leading from the keeper's dwelling to the light tower. Various repairs were made.

2

The First Keeper of the Marblehead Lighthouse

One of the first permanent settlers on the Marblehead Peninsula, Benajah Wolcott, was a Revolutionary War veteran, surveyor, and farmer who was born in New Haven, Connecticut on April 7, 1764. On June 26, 1822, at the age of fifty-eight, he was appointed the first keeper of the Marblehead Lighthouse by Stephen Pleasanton, Fifth Auditor of the United States Treasury, in charge of lighthouses. A resident of Danbury, Connecticut, and later New York, Wolcott came to the Western Reserve area of Ohio shortly after the 1796 expedition of Moses Cleaveland, who lived up to the spirit of his Old Testament name, organized the Connecticut Land Company, and lead New Englanders to the "Promised Land" along the shore of Lake Erie.

In 1806, Wolcott signed on as a member of the Firelands Survey Team. This area had been set aside for Connecticut families who had been burned out of their homes at the hands of the British Loyalists during the Revolutionary War.

Returning east in 1809, he brought his wife, Elizabeth (Bradley); two daughters, Phoebe and Selina; son, William; and two hired men, Osborn and Bishop back with him to the Ohio country. They left Connecticut on February 13, 1809, arriving sometime in March at the northern terminus of the Cuyahoga River. They made the arduous trip to their new home by sleigh. Since Lake Erie was covered with ice, Wolcott left his family in Cleaveland (the name was changed sometime later when a clerk dropped the "a") and continued on with the two hired men to the Marblehead Peninsula, where he intended to set up a farm. In May, he returned to Cleaveland for his family. They came by schooner, *Sally of Cuyahoga,* to Rocky Point, as Marblehead was then known.

In 1809, Wolcott built a small log cabin where the family lived for several years. It was close to the location of today's old stone house on Bayshore Road. They had already lived there before the declaration of war against the British and the surrender of General William Hull to the British at Detroit. Life was uncertain and potentially dangerous for the few inhabitants of the area because of the fear of attacks by Indians who, before this time, had, for the most part, been friendly but who had allied themselves with the British.

Just a few hundred yards west of the Wolcott cabin, the initial skirmish of the War of 1812 occurred on September 29th of that year; the Ottawa Indians killed

Figure 2-1. *Benajah Wolcott's home on Bayshore Road about three miles from the Marblehead Lighthouse. He completed the house in 1822 for himself and his new bride, Rachel. The house was purchased by the Ottawa County Historical Society in 1989 and is being restored.* Photo by Pat Williamsen. Used by permission.

eight men. A plaque and a small monument surrounded by an iron fence mark the battle site today. The men who died were James S. Bills, Simon Blackman, Mathew Guy, Alexander Mason, Daniel Mingus, Equilla Putney, Valentine Ramsdell, and Abraham Simonds. The historical marker known as the Giddings Monument describes the battle: "The first War of 1812 battle on Ohio soil was fought here when about 60 exhausted citizen soldiers were ambushed by about 130 Indians on September 29th. Twenty men held the Indians at bay in a cabin until the main body escaped by boat to Cedar Point. Two days later the defenders were rescued. Forty Indians, including several chiefs and eight Americans were killed in the skirmish, neither a victory nor a defeat for either side."

Forty-five years later, United States Senator Joshua R. Giddings, a sixteen-year-old boy at the time of the battle who had helped load rifles of the men who fought, returned to the area. He secured the site where he believed the men were buried and erected a monument and headstone. He remembered only three of the names. Some years later with the help of Mrs. Ross Cherry, author of *Blockhouses and Military Posts of the Firelands,* they revealed the other names.

Skirmishes between the settlers and the Indians continued quite regularly on the Peninsula. Many on both sides were killed; one of the settlers killed was Bishop who had come to the area with Benajah Wolcott. Many settlers had fled the Peninsula in 1812 by boat to Ogontz Place (Sandusky), Vermilion, and Huron; Osborn, who had been one of Benajah Wolcott's hired men, returned to Cleveland as did others. Reminiscing in the *Firelands Pioneer* (1870) about the fleeing of settlers, Horace Ramsdell, who had come to the Peninsula in 1811 with his parents and three brothers and had two boats, the *Swan* and the *Eliza*, narrated some of his experiences:

> When the settlers fled from the Peninsula in 1812, we took some of them down the shore to Vermillion and elsewhere in our boat. After this was done, we took our boat and Capt. Austin's and went back to the Orchards (as this area of the Peninsula was then called) to bring away some hemp. Thompson & Co. of Buffalo had stored there 50 tons of hemp which they had brought from Delaware, Ohio, by way of Fremont; while there, and just as we were leaving, some soldiers

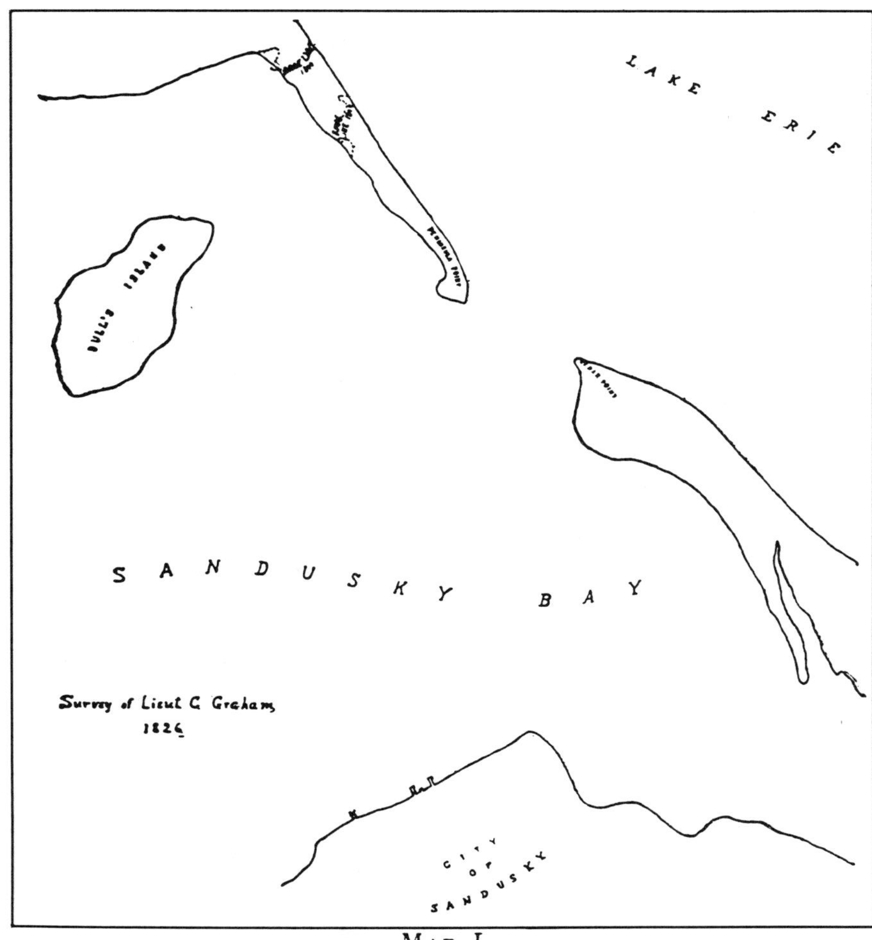

MAP I.

Figure 2-2. *1826 map shows Cedar Point and Peninsula Point (now Bay Point) to be about 3,000 feet apart. From* Lake Erie Floods, Lake Levels and Northeast Storms, *by Edwin Lincoln Moseley.* Courtesy of the Ohio Historical Society.

landed at the orchards. They were from Huron, and came in a scow to get fruit, &c. They set one man, named Guy, as a sentinel to keep watch while the others gathered apples. He stuck his gun into the ground by the bayonet, and climbed into an apple tree from the fence. As I passed him, going to the boat, I told him he was a pretty guard: if there were any Indians about there, they would steal his gun and shoot him before he knew it. He

> swore he was not afraid; he could get his gun before the Indian could. We started away with the hemp and left the soldiers there, and Guy still in the tree near the water. I was rowing the boat, and when only a few rods away, as I sat looking toward the orchard, I saw a puff of smoke, heard the report of a gun, and saw the soldiers drop from the trees as though they had all been shot, and throwing their things hither and thither, they made for their boat. Guy fell, shot through the forehead, and it was said that he was shot with the charge in his own gun, by an Indian.

During this period the Americans, the British, and the Indians were battling for supremacy in this backwoods of the new nation. General William Henry Harrison (later to become President Harrison) had fought the Indians, who had been supplied with arms by the British, and defeated them in 1811 at Tippecanoe. The Indian leader was the legendary Tecumseh. On August 16, 1812 the American General William Hull surrendered at Detroit to the British. His surrender, documented as one of the most ignominious defeats in American history, understandably alarmed the residents of the Marblehead Peninsula, who having heard the cannonading at Detroit, received no news of whether the Americans had won or lost. When the residents saw vessels loaded with men approaching the Peninsula's shore, they concluded they were invading British soldiers or Indians and that Hull had been defeated. The "invaders" turned out to be Americans in transports who had been paroled by Hull's surrender.

Fearful for their lives, many families who had settled on the Peninsula pulled up stakes and fled. Among them were the families of Benajah Wolcott, Epaphraditus Bull, Joseph Ramsdell, and Abaither

Sherley. Thirteen families made their way to Ogontz Place (Sandusky), taking shelter in Garrison's old log trading house. In addition to these families, the list, probably incomplete, included Charles Peck, H. Patch, Saunders with his wife and twin babies, Major Parsons, Bishop, Dr. Parks, (a practicing physician), Herrick, Cooper, Woolsey (a hired man, carpenter, and joiner), Col. P.P. Ferry (acting customs collector), and Ezra Lee.

Many of the families, including the Wolcotts, moved to Newburgh, a settlement on the Cuyahoga River. There Benajah's wife, Elizabeth, died of "miasmas," a common ailment of the settlers and characterized by chills and fever. Also a victim of the malady was Bull, a serious loss to the little band of settlers. Eventually some of the settlers of the Peninsula returned to their old homes, but others went to Vermilion, Huron, and other places; some returned to Cleveland. The defeat of the British by Oliver Hazard Perry on a hazy September afternoon in 1813 at Put-In-Bay very likely saved the Great Lakes for the Americans, opening vital inland waterways for the young United States.

Wolcott returned to the Peninsula with his children, ages seventeen, fifteen, and five. His eldest daughter, Phoebe, married Truman Pettibone (a native of Vermont) in Newburgh in 1815. When he returned sometime after 1814, Benajah Wolcott found many of the farms ravaged by desperadoes and marauding Indians but his cabin was still standing, probably because of his friendship with the Wyandot Chief, Ogontz.

His financial situation had become less desperate because of the pension he had requested as a soldier during the Revolutionary War, and received from the U.S. Government on October 1, 1819. On March 10, 1822, he married Rachel Miller, a Sandusky school teacher and daughter of John and Ann Miller of Chappelle Creek near Vermilion. Hector Kilbourn,

Justice of the Peace for Huron County, Ohio, stated, "I do hereby certify that I did on the tenth day of March last joining together Benajah Wolcott & Rachel Miller both of Perkins Township in Huron County in the holy estate of Matrimony." *April 24th, 1822.*

Entries made on the Port of Cuyahoga Marine List of 1818 confirmed the fact that families were returning to the Marblehead Peninsula: July 11, Schooner *Firefly,* D.B. Norton, touched from Buffalo to Danbury, landed families and household furniture; July 14, Schooner *Wasp*, Elam Crane, touched from Buffalo to Danbury, landed families; August 29, Sloop *Leopard,* Z. Wellman for Danbury. (*Note:* Could this be Zalmon Wildman? Wildman and Epaphraditus Bull were large landholders on the Marblehead Peninsula; "Wellman" might, actually, have been incorrectly entered for "Wildman.")

On June 24, 1822, Benajah Wolcott was appointed keeper of the newly completed Marblehead Lighthouse. A sum of $5,000 had been appropriated by the federal government for its construction and an additional $6,520 was provided for the keeper's dwelling. The "keeper's dwelling" referred to in the government appropriation statement and in Wolcott's acceptance of the lighthouse and dwelling was to be a home for he keeper on the lighthouse grounds.

Merlin Wolcott, a descendant of Benajah, wrote:

> Benajah's home on the Bay Shore, near the monument marking the place of the Battle of the Peninsula, was completed in 1822. The year is carved on the stone step at the front entrance. My impression is that Benajah built the house himself for his new bride.... It seems doubtful the Federal Government would have built the lighthouse keeper's house on private property on Benajah's farm that is some distance from the Lighthouse. In a certificate of acceptance of the Federal property

> in his possession, Benajah signed for "a Lighthouse, Dwelling house, Kitchen and necessary out house thereon erected, finished and in complete order...." signed in the presence of Truman Pettibone and Stephen Woolverton.

The keeper's dwelling built at the lighthouse would have been used primarily during the months navigation was open on the lakes and the light was functioning. Stephen Pleasanton, the Fifth Auditor of the Treasury, was well known as a penny-pinching beaurocrat with little knowledge of navigation. It is unlikely that he would have authorized the building of a dwelling on Benajah Wolcott's farm. It appears that Wolcott had two dwelling places: One was the stone house on Bayshore Road which he built, and the other at the lighthouse built by the federal government. We know that Benajah's family occupied the old stone house on Bayshore Road for some years after his death.

In a taped interview, the late Hilda Kelly Nelson, a Wolcott descendant, recounted the story of the wedding of Benajah's granddaughter, Elizabeth Pettibone, and John Reid Kelly, son of one of the builders of the lighthouse, William Kelly, at the old stone house on July 23, 1835.

> It seems that in those days the ministers were circuit riders, and if a couple wanted to get married they had to wait until the preacher came along. One day when Eliza was washing clothes in the yard, John arrived and said to her, "Today is our day. We're going to get married in a few minutes because the preacher is on his way." Eliza promptly took her hands out of the soapsuds, put on her new calico dress she had been saving for the occasion, and they were married in front of the fireplace in the old stone house.

The old stone house has been erroneously referred to as "the old stone fort." Except for a period of time in the 1920s when it was an eating place and a kitchen was added, it had been a family home. The last occupants were Lewis and Germaine Keller and their sons; Keller was a commercial fisherman on Lake Erie. In 1989, the Ottawa County Historical Society purchased the property from the Keller heirs; several years later, it was placed on the National Register of Historic Places. The stone house, built of limestone from an early quarry a short distance from the back of the house, is, undoubtedly, one of the oldest structures in Northwestern Ohio and an example of the early domestic architecture of the Firelands. Because of the Society's preservation and restoration, it will eventually be the focus of the rich history of the area and the lives of many of the families who lived on the Marblehead Peninsula.

For the pioneer families of the Peninsula there were both good times and hardships. Benajah often played the fiddle to provide music for dances. In 1815, he was invited to play for an Independence Day celebration in Cleveland and asked his youngest daughter, Selina, to accompany him. He, with his violin under his arm, and she, with her best gown, rode their horses to the east point of the Peninsula, where they took a canoe across and, swimming their horses behind them, crossed over the Bay to Cedar Point. There they mounted their horses and rode through the woods via the trail to Huron and Cleveland, swimming across streams when they came to them.

Crossing Sandusky Bay from the "east point" to Cedar Point, carrying a fiddle and a fancy ball gown and swimming the horses across, would seem highly unlikely today; however, an early map of the area shows that "east point," known today as Bay Point, extended far out into the Bay as did Cedar Point on the opposite shore. Benajah and his daughter, Selina, would have had to cross a fairly narrow channel, much smaller than the mouth of Sandusky Bay as we know it today.

Professor Edwin L. Moseley, who taught at Sandusky High School and Bowling Green State Normal School (later Bowling Green State University), described the changes over the years in lake levels and shorelines in his presidential address to the Ohio Academy of Science in 1904. He stated:

> Map I taken from a U.S. Government Chart, shows Peninsula Point as it was in 1826. The distance between it and Cedar Point was about 3,000 feet, but the water off the end of Peninsula Point was so shallow that when lowered by drouth and wind the distance from point to point was much less. H.A. Lyman, the old lighthouse keeper, told me he had seen the water so low that he thought the distance across was only about 300 feet. The Indians used to swim ponies across and B.F. Dwelle, who lived until 1902, and many other of the early settlers on the Marblehead Peninsula crossed in the same way, but not after 1830.

Even though there are no details of Benajah Wolcott's career as a lighthouse keeper, there is an indication that he assumed the duties before the official appointment. Note the following information from the diary of a Methodist minister, on June 17 1822, five days after he had left Black Rock (near Buffalo):

> The wind and storm abated. Our voyage having been longer than we expected, and the wind being still contrary, the captain of the vessel, notwithstanding his engagement, refused to take me to Portland (Sandusky), and after receiving my last money for the passage he set me ashore with

> four others on the peninsula west of Sandusky Bay and six miles opposite Portland. Here was a lighthouse, and besides the man who kept it there were no other inhabitants in that part of the peninsula. It was now after sunset, and during the last forty hours I had eaten but one meal, which was given me by the captain of the vessel. The man who kept the lighthouse had but little provisions with him; so without food I lay down on the floor and closed my eyes to sleep, hoping to forget my hunger. When the others had fallen asleep the keeper brought me a cracker and some milk, which I received with thanksgiving. Next morning the sun rose with splendor and I walked out to view the surrounding scenery.

Keeper of the lighthouse until his death on August 11, 1832 at the age of sixty-eight, Wolcott, it is said, died assisting in the burial of cholera victims; his son, William, died about the same time. Wolcott's grave site and headstone are in the family cemetery a short distance from the old stone house. The U.S. Treasury Department appointed Benajah's widow, Rachel, keeper of the Lighthouse on October 25, 1832, thereby becoming the first female lighthouse keeper on the Great Lakes.

Figure 2-3. *Paul Moon and his daughter, Elisabeth, direct descendants of Benajah Wolcott, with a hand-hewn rocker crib which reportedly cradled the infant Benajah in his native Connecticut. The gift came from Ann (Wolcott) Martinez of San Juan, Puerto Rico, a member of the Society of Descendants of Henry Wolcott, the first Wolcott to come to this continent in the 1600s.* Photo courtesy of *The Sandusky Register*.

3

Men and Women Who Kept the Light

In the early days, lighthouse keepers often held their jobs until old age or death overtook them. Many times, their wives and sometimes their children took over the work at the lighthouse and their wives were often appointed keepers following the deaths of their husbands. For instance, following Benajah Wolcott's death, his wife, Rachel, was appointed keeper by the U.S. Treasury Department on October 25, 1832.

There are no records of how she not only managed to take care of her home, the gardens and livestock, and her family, but also how she kept the light burning. Since her two children by Benajah, Henry and Elizabeth, were about five- and six-years old, they were too young to be of much help. Her stepson, William Wolcott, son of Benajah and his first wife, Elizabeth

Figure 3-1. *The lighthouse and the keeper's house as they appeared circa 1910. The house is standing today and is being renovated.* Photo courtesy of the Great Lakes Historical Society.

Bradley, died in 1832, about the same time his father's death occurred; perhaps he, too, was a cholera victim. Phoebe Wolcott, daughter of Benajah and Elizabeth, had married Truman Pettibone in Newburgh, Ohio, in 1815 and had returned to the Peninsula; their five children were Bradley, William, Nancy, Elizabeth, and Albert. It is likely that this family assisted Rachel in keeping the lighthouse running and in doing the chores at the old stone house.

Selina Wolcott, the second daughter of Benajah and Elizabeth, had married John Ramsdell in 1817 and moved to Bloomingville in 1825. John and Selina had five sons. After John's death, she moved back to the Danbury Peninsula and married her widowed brother-in-law, Jacob Ramsdell, who had two sons and five daughters. The Ramsdell family may also have helped Rachel keep the light.

In addition to the household and gardening chores (lighthouse keepers had to have gardens and livestock for their daily subsistence), they had many other duties. They had to keep the light burning, clean and polish the lens, clean and fill the lamp, trim the wicks or replace them, and clean the copper and brass fixtures of the apparatus as well as the utensils used in the lantern and watchroom. They had to clean the walls, floors, balconies, and galleries, sweep and dust the spiral stairways, landings, doors, windows, and window recesses and passageways from the lantern to the oil storage area. Besides their regular duties, they often rescued and aided people who were victims of treacherous storms. The rocky promontory at the mouth of Sandusky Bay, where the Marblehead Lighthouse stands guard, is considered one of the stormiest places on Lake Erie.

Little is known about Rachel's activities during her years as lighthouse keeper because no records have been located, yet there is clear evidence that when she was appointed to take Benajah's place on October 25, 1832, she was the first female lighthouse keeper on the Great Lakes. Rachel, whose parents were John and Ann Miller, was born at Chappelle Creek (Vermilion); this young schoolteacher from Sandusky must have had a difficult and lonely life on the sparsely populated Peninsula. Sadder still, she received no recognition for the role she played in keeping the Marblehead Lighthouse in operation.

After two years of widowhood and serving as lighthouse keeper, Rachel married Jeremiah Van Benschoten,

Figure 3-2. *Captain Charles Hunter (left) and Assistant Keeper Edward Herman, with Hunter's grandson Mills Brandes circa 1924.* Photo courtesy of Mills Brandes.

a widower from Vermilion whose wife, Sarah Wetherlow, had died in 1833. Jeremiah, who had come with his parents from Dutchess County, New York to Huron County, Ohio when married to Sarah, lived in a blockhouse as a protection against marauding Indians who were offered money by the British for American scalps. He took part in the township's first election in 1811. After Hull's surrender to the British at Detroit in 1812, many of the settlers left the frontier lakeshore; even though the Van Benschoten family retreated by boat several times to Rocky River, they eventually returned, settling on Lot 20, Section 14 in Vermilion.

According to the Van Benschoten genealogy, Jeremiah was a hunter, trapper,and farmer:

> He witnessed flights of wild pigeons which darkened the sky for an entire day. They flew so low they could be struck down by poles. He also witnessed the migration of grey and black squirrels which swam down the Huron River headed east, bent on going east and nothing would stop them; they were as fanatical as the Crusaders. They were in great mass and days in passing.

Jeremiah was appointed lighthouse keeper on February 14, 1834. No official records have been located describing the eight years that he and Rachel tended the light; however, the Van Benschoten genealogy recorded several activities that took place there:

> It was here that Hezekiah Darrow once came to buy a team of Indian ponies of him. They reviewed the herd but could not come to terms. Two of the ponies, Darrow recalled, were disemboweled by leaping on to the pickets of the barnyard fence in their efforts. The ponies were extremely wild–had never known any restraint.

Figure 3-3. *"Cap" Hunter had many hobbies. One was making yarn pictures of his favorite subjects.* Photo courtesy of Mills Brandes.

Possibly, the last battle to take place between the Canadians and the Americans had its denouement at the Marblehead Lighthouse during the time Jeremiah and Rachel were keepers. In what is known as "The Battle of Pelee Island," a group calling themselves "Patriots," but referred to by the Pelee Islanders as "Fenians," invaded across the ice from Sandusky and attempted to take control of the island on February 26, 1838. The battle was part of an uprising against the "Family Compact" rule in Upper Canada. After some fighting, part of which took place on the ice, the "Patriots" retreated across the frozen lake to the Marblehead Peninsula, where they passed the night in the lighthouse and in and about Jeremiah's house and outbuildings. They were taken prisoner by the Ohio Militia on March 4, 1838.

After Jeremiah and Rachel had kept the light for eight years, Jeremiah returned to his old blockhouse in Huron County. It is not known whether he and Rachel were divorced or separated. Having died there on March 12, 1856, toward the end of a long and severe winter, he was buried in Berlin Heights. A son, Samuel Wetherlow Van Benschoten, ran the home farm while his father was at the lighthouse.

The next keeper of the Marblehead Light was Roderick Williston, who was appointed on August 4, 1841 and served until 1843, according to records in the National Archives. Even though Williston's lighthouse log has not been located, it is commonly known that activity on the Lake and the Bay would suggest that he must have been busy because Sandusky Bay was, at that time, considered one of the best harbors on the Great Lakes. Commerce flourished and the beginnings of passenger service by boat created much activity that grew through several decades. According to Gordon Wendt, author of *In the Wake of the Walk-In-The-Water*:

> The earliest service on record was to Lower Sandusky (Fremont) in 1822. Boats were the horse boats *Car of Sandusky* and *Pegasus*. They were barges propelled by treadmills operated by horses. The first steamer on the run was *Maj. Jack Downing* in 1834, with *Water Witch* serving later in the year. These small sidewheelers used Hollister's pier which was the west pier at Wayne Street. In 1843, the *Gen. Vance* was on the route, which by now also included the various landings on the north shore of

the Bay, in counter-clockwise sequence: Molitor's, Fox's, Hartshorn's Boschen's, Dwelle's, Presque Isle and Plaster Bed (Gypsum). The route then continued up the Bay to Lower Sandusky.

Charles F. Drake (1791-1876) succeeded Williston as lighthouse keeper and served for approximately seven years starting in 1843. He is listed in the 1870 census as a lighthouse keeper, 73 years of age, with a wife, Mary, age 63. Drake, described as "an eccentric gentleman of the old school," lived for a time in Bloomingville where he conducted a store in partnership with Samuel Caldwell. At one time, he was the proprietor of a tavern in Sandusky known as the "Portland House at the Sign

Figure 3-4*. Limestone quarries comprise the interior of the Marblehead Peninsula. Quarrying began with the earliest residents of the Peninsula and continues today.* [Postcard from the author's collection.]

Figure 3-5. *Quarry owners built docks from which to ship limestone throughout the Great Lakes. Doner's Dock and quarry were located on Sandusky Bay near the present site of the Marina Restaurant.* Postcard from the author's collection.

of the Golden Lamb." At one time, Drake was the lighthouse keeper on Green Island several miles west of South Bass Island in Lake Erie. On New Year's Eve, 1864, when the Green Island Lighthouse was destroyed by fire, Drake, his wife, and daughter survived by huddling together under feather ticks. When his son, Pitt, who was attending a New Year's Eve dance at Doller's Hall at Put-In-Bay, saw the flames, he attempted to reach the lighthouse but a severe winter storm prevented him and his friends from crossing to Green Island until the next morning when they rescued the family who suffered from burns and below zero degree weather exposure.

Figure 3-6. *Johnson's Island was used mostly for farming and limestone quarrying until the turn of the century. The first owner was Epaphraditus Bull. In 1852 it was sold to Leonard Johnson who, in 1861, leased it to the government for use as a prison for captured Confederate soldiers*. Postcard from the author's collection.

In the 1840s, while Drake was keeper of the Marblehead Light, Sandusky became the center of railroad activity. The city had lost a long, bitter battle with the Ohio Canal Commissioners to become the northern terminus of a central canal. Instead, two canals were built: the Ohio and Erie Canal in Eastern Ohio, and the Miami and Erie Canal in Western Ohio. A vigorous opponent to Sandusky's bid for the canal was Alfred Kelley (no relation to John Kelly, builder of the Marblehead Lighthouse). Alfred, who was known as the "father of the canal system," owned land along the Cuyahoga River where the Ohio and Erie Canal eventually terminated. When his brothers, Irad and Datus, took over Cunningham's Island, they renamed it Kelleys Island. A contemporary of Colonel Drake, Oran Follett, a prominent Sandusky resident, was instrumental in turning the focus away from canals and securing the city as the center of railroad activity. Establishment of the northern terminus of the only north and south railroad, together with Sandusky's strategic location on one of the best harbors on the Great Lakes, promised a future of both rail and water commerce. Follett's home on Wayne Street is now the Follett House Museum.

Captain Lodavick Brown became the next keeper of the Marblehead Lighthouse, but the dates of his service are not known. From incomplete records, it can be assumed that he served for approximately four years. From *William's History of Erie and Huron Counties,* we learn that Hubbard Hollister and Lodavick Brown

Figures 3-7. *Johnson's Island was the site of a prison camp for Confederate soldiers during the Civil War. On September 19, 1864, a plot to free the prisoners was attempted at the time Thomas Dyer was the lighthouse keeper. Only reminder of that era is the beautifully maintained Confederate Cemetery on Johnson's Island.* Postcard from the author's collection.

came to Perkins Township in 1821; Mr. Hollister purchased the Dillingham farm in an area known as the "Yankee Settlement" because its inhabitants who had come from Connecticut were part of the exodus from that state to the Firelands Western Reserve.

The next keeper, Jared B. Keyes (1815-1891), a seafaring man from New York State, was appointed in 1853. In 1834, he married Arvilla Knapp Wolcott, a native of Vermont and the widow of William Wolcott, a soldier who was the son of Benajah Wolcott and his first wife, Elizabeth Bradley. In what was one of the first weddings to take place at the Marblehead Lighthouse, Jared and Arvilla's daughter, Alvira, married William Alexander Clemons on January 1, 1856. William and Alvira's home is still standing at the first bend of the road toward the lighthouse.

One of the responsibilities of lighthouse keepers was to aid mariners in distress. Captain Keyes was able to rescue two survivors when the barge *Empire*, with a

Figure 3-8. *Looking east from the fort, Johnson's Island, O.* Postcard from author's collection.

Figure 3-9. *Block house Johnson's Island, O.* Postcard from the author's collection.

crew of eleven men, was wrecked off Marblehead Point. The *Empire*, from Port Dover, Canada, was bound from Toledo to Tonawanda, New York, with a cargo of timber. In her unpublished paper, Marie Wonnell described the rescue:

> Mr. Keyes recruited eight volunteers to man the life boat and rescue the men who were clinging to the rigging of the vessel. Among the volunteers were his son, Robert, and his son-in-law, William Clemons. When the life boat hit the breakers, the steering oar broke and the men were landed end-over-end on the beach. Securing new oars, they launched the boat from another part of the beach,

Figure 3-10. *Magazine and section of fort Johnson's Island, O.* Postcard from author's collection.

and succeeded in fastening a line from the vessel to the shore. But by that time the exhausted sailors had been washed away one by one, until only the captain and one seaman were required to be rescued. The newspaper account praised the two heroic mothers, Mrs. Keyes and Mrs. Clemons, who built a fire on shore and waited with dry clothing, flannels, and "restoratives" for the survivors.

During the Keyes' administration, the Marblehead Light was refitted with a fourth-order Fresnel lens (a single lamp surrounded by rings of prismatic glass arranged to refract and direct the light rays to increase their intensity). The fixed white light had a visibility range of 12 miles.

The *Ottawa Democrat* of November 26, 1858 stated:

> Capt. Borden informs us that we were in error last week in stating Mr. Keyes was "removed." We are now informed that he resigned. We correct the error with pleasure as it is but justice to our friend Keyes.

In the June, 1860 Danbury Township, Ottawa County census, D.L. Dayton was listed as a lighthouse keeper, 45 years of age, and a native of Vermont. His 28-year-old wife was a native of New York, and they had two children, Amelia and George L., listed as three years old and three-and-half years old, respectively. No other information has been found about Dayton, who evidently served as keeper of the Marblehead Lighthouse from 1859 until 1861.

During the Civil War, the keeper was Thomas Dyer, who was appointed on March 29, 1861 at a salary of $350 per year. He and his wife, Louisa, came to Ohio from Connecticut where he was born in 1796 and she in 1799. They had two children, John and Elizabeth. According to Marie Wonnell's research, the area around the lighthouse at this time was still very primitive; since there was no road to the lighthouse, Mrs. Dyer made a path through the woods by white-washing the tree trunks so that their children could find the way to school.

Even though the Marblehead Peninsula was far removed from the battlefields of the Civil War, one event took place which brought the conflict close. A few miles from the Lighthouse and within sight of it, Johnson's Island was the location of the 300-acre Confederate Prison Camp, which housed more than 10,000 officers captured in battle far to the south. A plot to free the prisoners was attempted on September 19, 1864, when a group of Confederate sympathizers armed with revolvers and bowie knives took passage on the steamer *Philo Parsons*, which they seized at Kelleys Island. They then set out for Middle Bass

Figure 3-11. *The steamer, ISLAND QUEEN, was taken over by Confederate sympathizers at Middle Bass Island in their plot to free the prisoners on Johnson's Island.* Courtesy of the Institute for Great Lakes Research, Bowling Green State University.

Island, where they met and took over the *Island Queen*, another passenger boat which they sank after discharging the passengers. At Middle Bass they awaited the signal, a rocket to be fired from the U.S. gunboat *Michigan*, which they were to board and capture.

Because the rocket was never set off, the scheme proved to be a fiasco when the U.S. Provost Marshal in Detroit sent warnings to the authorities in Sandusky. Charles H. Cole, a Confederate agent who had been living in Sandusky, had planned the elaborate scheme which included a dinner on board the *Michigan* with ship's officers and guests from Sandusky who were to be paralyzed with drugged champagne. Cole was arrested at his hotel in the afternoon, and the conspirators on the *Philo Parsons* (under the leadership of John Yates Beall) set sail back to Detroit, where they scuttled the steamer and escaped into Canada.

Remaining lighthouse keeper until his death on December 12, 1865, Dyer was followed by Russell Douglas, a native of Nova Scotia. He served from 1865 to 1872, when he retired at age 71 due to old age. The next keeper, Thomas J. Keyes, served only 11 months before resigning in 1873. Information on Douglas and Keyes was included in a report dated July 7, 1938, and submitted to the Superintendent of Lighthouses at Buffalo, New York by Edward M. Herman, then assistant keeper.

The next appointed lighthouse keeper, George H. McGee, served from 1873 to 1896. When he died at age 45, he was succeeded by his wife, Johanna. Mrs. McGee was appointed keeper on July 8, 1896, and served until her retirement on March 16, 1903. Including the time she assisted her husband, Mrs. McGee had been in the lighthouse service over 30 years, possibly longer than any other person in the United States.

The lighthouse log kept by the McGees was located by Marblehead residents Ervin Mutach and Rosemary Merckens, and given to the Center for Archival Collections at Bowling Green State University, in 1986. (See the next chapter on "The Keeper's Log" for appropriate excerpts from the journal.)

Major changes occurred at the lighthouse during the time the McGees and their family kept the light. The height of the lighthouse was increased by 15 feet, the old lantern was replaced by one from Erie, Pennsylvania, and a clock-like mechanism was installed to make a 10-second flashing signal. A large Fresnel lens, ordered from Paris, was installed after it had been exhibited at the St. Louis World's Fair.

Charles A. Hunter, known as "Cap" Hunter, became the next keeper in 1903. He served until his retirement in 1933, the year after the death of his wife, Elizabeth. The son of a naval officer and shipowner, "Cap" spent his youth on the Great Lakes. Before he was transferred to Marblehead, he manned the lighthouse at Buffalo, New York. His grandson, Mills Brandes of Marblehead, recalled living at the lighthouse with his grandparents from 1922 until 1929 and attending school at the old Marblehead grade school, now the Schoolhouse Gallery. Hunter died in 1938.

Although lighthouse keepers are often viewed as reclusive individuals who value their solitude, "Cap" Hunter certainly did not fit that profile. During the navigation season, he tended the light which had, by this time, been converted to electricity; a revolving light with a 300 watt bulb flashed 42,000 candlepower for a distance of 16 miles over the lake. He played host to thousands of visitors to the lighthouse, spinning yarns and telling stories of Lake Erie's fierce storms, the wreck of the *Consuelo,* and the awarding of the U.S. Lifesaving Medal to the Clemons brothers, (Ai, Lucien and Hubbard) for their daring rescue of survivors. From the top of the lighthouse, he would point out the world's largest limestone quarry and the country's shortest passenger railroad.

An expert with tools, he practiced woodworking and taught the first manual training class in the Marblehead schools. A few miles from the lighthouse, he built a house (on the shore) of timbers from the wreck of an old barge. He designed and made colorful yarn tapestry pictures of the lighthouse, ships, and local scenes; he also wrote short stories and published the words for a song entitled "The Lighthouse By The Bay."

Hunter, who retired in 1933, was succeeded by Edward Herman, who had been the assistant keeper since 1913. He served until 1943, when the Coast Guard became responsible for the operation of the Marblehead Lighthouse. The Hermans lived in the upstairs apartment of the keeper's dwelling. The last full-time keeper of the Marblehead Lighthouse, he died in 1964. According to his records, the station had been manned by a keeper and an assistant from 1903 until 1913. Assistant keepers preceding Herman were Clinton Egleton, who was in service two months; Charles E. Perry, from June 4, 1903 to October 10, 1906; and Earl Mapes from October 11, 1906, to October 1, 1913.

Like the weather on Lake Erie, the administration of lighthouses in the United States has a long and stormy history. In 1790, the Revenue Cutter Service, established by the federal government, was a sort of floating police service. In 1915, it merged with the Lifesaving Service, which had begun in 1848. The Great Lakes did not have a Lifesaving Service until 1876; in that year, Captain Lucien Monroe Clemons was appointed first keeper at the Marblehead Lifesaving Station. When it opened, the Lifesaving Service was under the U.S. Treasury Department; in 1915, President Woodrow Wilson signed an act combining the Lifesaving Service with the Revenue Cutter Service, and thus forming the U.S. Coast Guard. It remained under the Treasury Department until 1967, when it was transferred to the Department of Transportation. During World War II, the Coast Guard became a part of the U.S. Navy; after the war, the Coast Guard returned to its original role as the protector of life and property on the waterways.

Since 1942, the Coast Guard has been responsible for the operation of lighthouses, buoys, and other aids to navigation in the United States. Coast Guard personnel from the Marblehead Coast Guard Station took over the responsibility of keeping the Marblehead Lighthouse in 1943. Today the beacon is maintained by the Aids to Navigation Team in Huron, Ohio.

Figure 3-12. *The United States Lifesaving Service was established in 1876. In that year, Captain Lucien Monroe Clemons was appointed first keeper of the Marblehead Lifesaving Station. Spectators often gathered to watch the lifesaving drills.* Postcard from the author's collection.

4

The Keeper's Log

The day-to-day life of the lighthouse keeper and his family can best be told in the keeper's own words—in this case, the log kept by George H. McGee and his wife, Johanna. Mr. McGee, who was appointed keeper in 1872, served until his death at age 45 in 1896. His widow, Johanna, was appointed keeper and she served until 1903 when she retired. According to the *Elmore Tribune* of January 15, 1903:

> The Marblehead lighthouse is to be equipped with the latest improved flash light and new lens ... Mrs. J. H. McGee, keeper, has been in the lighthouse service over 30 years, longer than any other person in the United States, she will be supplied with an assistant next year. The lighthouse is the second oldest on Lake Erie, the one at Ft. Erie near Buffalo is the oldest.

It was a common practice for the Lighthouse Service to appoint the widow of the deceased keeper at his death. For many years, there were no pensions or death compensations for lighthouse keepers so the remaining family often had no means of support; appointing the widow was often the humanitarian thing to do.

The lack of pensions created another problem. Frequently, keepers worked until they became too old or too weak to perform the duties required of them. It was not until 1919 that the Lighthouse Service provided a retirement pension system for keepers at age 65 and with 30 years of service.

The work of keeping the light burning in the days when lighthouses were manned was a family affair. Wives and children were involved in cultivating the garden, caring for livestock, maintaining the living quarters, and tending the light. In the days before electricity, the keeper's job included keeping the lamps in the tower filled and lit, polishing the brass, keeping the fuel tanks filled to proper levels, and cleaning and polishing the lenses. The keeper and his family were involved in the endless routine of painting, polishing, scrubbing, scouring, and swabbing. On August 30, 1873, George McGee wrote in his log:

> I finished work on the apparatus today. It has been a hard and dirty job.

A notation of the weather was made daily in the log, as well as the names of all the vessels that passed the lighthouse, the condition of the lake, and any unusual occurrences. Lighthouse keepers were responsible for aiding mariners in distress until, in 1876, the Life Saving Service (later the U.S. Coast Guard) was established on the Great Lakes and lighthouse keepers were relieved of that responsibility. Captain Lucien Clemons was

Figure 4-1. *Following a severe flood in 1974, the surface of the tower was severely damaged. A gunnite surfacing was applied after it was skinned, repointed, and put in condition for the sealing coat. The original stonework surface can be seen in this picture.* Photo courtesy of Neil and Rosemary Merckens.

appointed keeper of the Marblehead Life Saving Station on September 20, 1876.

Children of the Marblehead Lighthouse keepers were able to attend school nearby—a problem lighthouse families in remote areas often faced. Isolation, another common problem, evidently did not plague families living at the Marblehead station during the mid-1800s. The McGee log tells of attending dances in the area, campground meetings, fairs, and frequent trips to Sandusky. The latter was accomplished by rowing or sailing across the Bay, and traveling by passenger boats which connected the Marblehead Peninsula with Sandusky. On July 15, 1875, he recorded in the log:

> Went to Sandusky to take wife and children. Went in rowboat at 10:00 a.m., returned at 5:00 p.m.

On the first of each month, he went to Sandusky to draw his salary and to mail reports.

The following is not the complete log of George and Johanna McGee, nor is it all written by Mr. McGee. After his death, the log was kept by his wife and, judging from the content, some of it was written by his daughters. Minor changes were made in punctuation and spelling only when clarity was an issue. All names of vessels are capitalized.

The Lighthouse Keeper's Log (1873–1903)

August 27, 1873. Heavy gale and big sea, NE cool and cloudy, very dark this evening. Painted the COMET and worked at the apparatus until 3:00 P.M. Large quantity of lumber commenced coming ashore at the station and on the beach for a while on either side. I saved several hundred feet, it is estimated that twenty-two thousand feet have come ashore on Marblehead.

August 30. Light winds from every point of the compass today. Clear and scorching hot all day. Bright starlight evening. I finished work on the apparatus today. (It has been a hard and dirty job.) The Collector of Customs and wife paid this station a visit this afternoon.

September 8. Light changeable winds, cloudy, warm and moonlight tonight. I gave the top of the lantern a coat of red paint today. Carpenter worked all day on the barn.

September 9. Moderate easterly winds all day. Clear, warm and moonlight tonight. I gave the outside of the lantern a coat of coaltar today. Carpenter worked all day on the barn.

September 10. I gave the pedestal a coat of paint this a.m. I shingled 3/4 of a day on the barn.

September 11. I whitewashed the barn today.

September 30. IMPORTANT EVENT. This day I do not work for Uncle Sam. The only important event which transpired today was the birth of a daughter weighing 8 pounds at 2:00 P.M.

October 20. Cleaned fountains and burners. Scow A. HAND of Toledo went ashore 1 mile w of the lighthouse at 11 o'clock, she has become a total wreck and is being stripped of her outfit.

November 6. I went to Sandusky for supplies today. Col. Harwood, Mr. Mullenback and Cedar Point lightkeeper visited the station today.

November 12. Stayed at the station all day. Gale NW winds, freezing snow squalls all day.

Figure 4-2. *The additional 15 feet added to the tower in 1897 was of brick construction. The bricks can be seen in this picture.* Photo courtesy of Neil and Rosemary Merckens.

December 1. Fresh NE, heavy sea, snowy and light rain squalls all day and tonight. Revenue cutter passed down and went to Sandusky at 9 A.M. Cedar Point is not lit up tonight. Navigation closed at that port.

December 31. I went to Sandusky today at 8:30 A.M. to mail reports and draw salary and returned on Jan. 2 at 8 P.M.

March 12, 1874. This afternoon a small boat with 2 men went down the lake with the ice. The wind was fresh NW and current running about 4 miles per hour. Freezing hard.

April 10. Cleaned out the barn. Grubbing and burning stumps all day. Steam barge passed with a barge in tow at 4:00 P.M.

April 11. Went to Sandusky for oars and to sell the lumber which I picked up last fall. Fresh NNE rain A.M., heavy snow P.M.

April 13. Cleaned the lens and lantern glass today.

April 18. Pulled down 8 rods of rail fence and set out 2 grape vines.

April 14. Cleaned the Pedestal with emery paper, finished painting my boat which I have been building.

April 15. Set out 5 cherry trees.

June 4. Planting corn, sweet potatoes and tomatoes.

June 12. Coal tarred stairs, oil butt platforms. Drawed off 100 gal. butt, washed and scalded 50 gal. butt.

June 16. Cleaned brass on apparatus A.M. Steamer HAZE arrived with supplys at 2:00 P.M. and cleared at 5:00 P.M. Col. T. Harwood resigns and Col. Blunt succeeds.

June 25. Off in the country hunting my cow.

July 31. Coaltarred lantern floor and cleaned tower stairs.

August 31. Painted my boat this 31st day of August, 1874 in the state of Ohio, in the County of Ottawa, and the town of Danbury in the United States, boathouse situated on Marblehead Light Station in the State, County and the Township aforesaid mentioned. (Seal)

December 1. Sandusky Bay froze over yesterday. The lake is filled with floating ice.

December 11. Cedar Point did not light up tonight.

December 14. The lake is covered with ice. No open water to be seen.

January 1, 1875. Left the station at 5 A.M. for Sandusky to mail reports and draw salary, and did not return till Jan. 4th at 6:00 P.M.

February 22. Built rail fence from lake to barn.

February 23. Hauling stone for stone wall with team. 10 hrs.

February 24. Building stonewall—10 hrs.

February 25. " "

February 26. " "

February 27. " "

Figure 4-3. *The AMERICAN EAGLE, built in 1880 by John Monk of Sandusky for Andrew Wehrle of Middle Bass Island, was specially equipped for ice breaking. She ran among the islands in the summer and out of Sandusky in the winter. Here she is shown in ice surrounded by bicyclists.* Photo courtesy of the Institute for Great Lakes Research, Bowling Green State University.

April 27. Steamer HAZE passed up at 11:20 A.M. Came to anchor at Kelleys Island. Fresh NE.

April 29. Steamer HAZE came to Clemons dock at 5:30 A.M. Loaded stone barge, anchored and cleaned up at 1:00 P.M. Fearful gale NW. A scow dismasted her foremast about two miles E of this station. The water has been very low today breaking up shell rock at the foot of the boat storage.

May 1. A vessel sunk about 1 1/2 miles north of the station at 11:30 A.M. Gales NE A.M., S to W P.M., NW tonight. Rainy, 5 lives lost (schooner CONSUELO from Cleveland to Toledo with sandstone. 2 men rescued by LS Crew.)

June 19. Steamer GAZELLE layed the cable from Marblehead to Kelleys Island this P.M.

July 4. Attended W.A. Clemons dance last night.

July 8. Steamer HAZE stopped at this station at 7:50 P.M. and cleared at 8:30 P.M. Com. Doller, Capt. Davis (of the Lighthouse Board), J. McCarran inspected the station.

July 15. Went to Sandusky to take wife and children. Went in rowboat 10:00 A.M., returned at 5:00 P.M.

August 8. Went to camp meeting today and tonight.

August 10. Went to camp ground meeting at Put-In-Bay.

August 17. Went to Sandusky to see the Pound Boat Regatta.

August 25. Schooner MAYFLOWER sunk about 1 mile S of the W end of Kelleys Island. Loaded with stone.

September 5. Cleaned apparatus and fountains and burners.

September 6. Helped Sam Wilson thrash wheat and oats.

September 7. Helped Philip Smith thrash wheat and oats.

September 12. Cleaned lantern glass and tower.

September 23. Went to Erie County Fair 8:00 A.M. to 5:00 P.M.

October 3. Went to Wolcotts for hazelnuts.

October 30. Stmr. GERMANIA landed 6 tons of coal on the beach.

January 7, 1876. I extinguished the light this morning according to regulations.

January 12. The passage is full of ice.

February 23. Went to Wilsons dance last night.

March 10. Steamer GOLDEN EAGLE commenced running between the islands and Sandusky.

March 23. Supt. of Construction of Life Boat Houses was here this P.M.

April 1. Capt. John McCarran visited the station to inspect the site proposed for a Life Boat Station.

May 12. Whitewashed dining room, chicken coop and coal shed.

August 4. Steamer HAZE (new HAZE) came to anchor off this station at 12:30 P.M. and got underway at 3:00 P.M. Coms. Polter, Sampist and McKain inspected the station. Capt. McKenzie left the usual supplies.

May 2, 1877. Planted 1/2 bu each potatoes, cabbage, tomato pepper, peas and lettuce seed.

May 4. Set 10 raspberry roots (Clarks Red and Black Cap) also 10 currant bushes.

May 11, 1877. Lake Coast Survey Boat ADA came to anchor SE of station at sunrise and landed 25 officers and men to work on this coast. They all camped at Ward's Point.

June 3. Stmr. ADA moved survey camp from Marblehead to Kelleys Island this A.M.

June 4. Coal tarred tower stairs. Planted sugar beets.

August 30, 1878. Hotel burned at Put-In-Bay tonight.

September 2. Went to blacksmith's shop. 3 hrs.

March 28, 1879. Went to Sandusky 10 A.M. to 6 P.M. to purchase building materials.

April 30. Three masted schooner capsized in the passage between this station and Kelleys Island at 3 A.M. loaded with hickory butts. Crew taken off by yawl boat from a passing barge and taken to Sandusky by Life Boat No. 9. Gale NW. Tug MYSTIC is towing the wreck into Sandusky tonight.

September 2. Heavy gale with snow set in last night at 10:00 o'clock. Gale NE today. Three vessels came ashore last night between this station and the Life Boat Station. Tender HAZE came up the Lake. I went into Sandusky at noon.

December 2. Tugs MYTRLE and MYSTIC pulled Schooner NEW HAMPSHIRE off the beach this P.M. and towed her to Sandusky. She was one of the vessels which went ashore on the 20th of last month.

Figure 4-4. *The passenger steamer, A. WHERLE, JR., was built in 1889 in Sandusky. She was built for the Peninsula run covering Marblehead, Lakeside, Catawba, Cedar Point, and Put-In-Bay. She ended her days in 1932 as a club for the Cook County Democratic Party in Chicago.* Postcard from the author's collection.

February 10, 1880. Cedar Point relit tonight. Green Island has been lit for several nights.

May 5. The lights in this station went out between 2 o'clock this morning and sunrise. Trimmed at 11:00 last night. Looked at light from the dwelling at 2:00 o'clock. Cannot account for the accident. Dead calm last night.

May 24. U.S. Tender HAZE delivered supplies to this station this P.M. The lard oil lamps were taken down and mineral oil lamps substituted. Commander Bridgeman and Capt. D.P. Heap inspected the station.

September 17. Tender HAZE came to anchor at 3 P.M. and cleared for Sandusky at 7:30. Capt. G.W. Hayward (new inspector) inspected station. The crew landed several boat loads of building material for the new dwelling.

September 18. C.W. Channing came to station in a sailboat. P.M. went back to Sandusky.

September 20. C.W. Channing and laborers arrived P.M. and commenced excavating cellar for new dwelling.

October 5. Scow H.A. SAMMARS went ashore and sunk 1/2 mile NW of Lt. House P.M. in trying to get away from the dock.

October 8. Steam pump raised the SAMMARS, tug towed her off and placed her alongside the dock.

October 9. SAMMARS sunk alongside the dock last night.

July 2, 1881. President Garfield shot today.

September 19. President James A. Garfield died at Long Branch at 10:00 P.M. and buried at Cleveland Sept. 26.

September 26. Went to Cleveland to attend President Garfield's funeral. Left the station at 5 A.M. and returned at 5 P.M.

October 4. Commander Geo. W. Hayward, Capt. James Kanzia and Engineer Wall inspected the station. Library No. 261 containing 31 vols. was left at this station. This is the first library ever left here.

December 16. Discontinued the light at this station this morning. Cedar Point not lit tonight and Huron, Green Island, have not been seen for several nights on account of the snowy weather. No boats except the AMERICAN EAGLE have passed this station for 8 days. The lake is covered with ice and the ice on the bay is 7 and 8 inches thick.

March 25, 1882. Steamer GOLDEN EAGLE sunk by the ice in 24 feet.

April 1. Steamer GOLDEN EAGLE has been raised.

May 18. Steamer AMERICAN EAGLE exploded her boiler about 2 1/2 miles N of this station while racing with the Steamer JAY COOKE. Four of the crew were killed and all of the passengers badly scalded (two died–total 6.)

July 26, 1883. Drowned, George McGee, Jr., youngest son of George and Hannah McGee. Aged 17 months.

March 21, 1885. Today 118 teams passed this station with wine, fish, etc. from the Islands to Sandusky and return. Teams drawing heavy loads have been crossing from the Islands to Sandusky for the past nine weeks. The 118 teams counted today were those passing both ways. The mercury has indicated zero or below on thirty-three different days during the past winter. The ice on the Lake is from twenty to thirty inches in thickness, clear and solid. Several times the mercury indicated 16 degrees below zero.

March 23. About thirty teams passed the station on the ice today for Sandusky from the Islands. This will be the last of crossing as the cracks are opening.

March 26. This is the first day since last fall warm enough for the bees to fly. Mercury 56 degrees above zero.

April 25. A large field of ice passed down this P.M. Last of the season.

May 9. Heavy wind, rain, hail and snow squalls all day.

September 10. Heavy dead sea rolling on the beach this morning. NE. There has been no NE wind for several days. Yesterday the wind blew a gale NW. Last night the wind was light westerly and this A.M. SW. Fine misty rain last night and today. The surf rolled up on the grass.

February 16, 1886. Steamer AMERICAN EAGLE commenced running today.

April 2. Mr. Wisner arrived and ran the lines for the new fence.

April 3. The erection of a new fence commenced today.

April 19. Laborers finished the new iron fence today.

April 27. Mr. Schangler (Supt. of Construction) and son arrived at 4:00 P.M. to inspect the new fence. Will leave at 6 A.M. tomorrow.

January 26, 1887. Stmr. AMERICAN EAGLE commenced running today.

January 28. EAGLE broke her wheel in the ice near Kelleys Island.

January 29. Exhibited the light at this station for the EAGLE last night. She was delayed in coming out of the Bay yesterday P.M. and did not arrive at Marblehead until dark. She layed to on anchor until daylight this morning about 1/2 mile SE of this station.

March 7. Steamer NORMA and tug ANNIE ROBERTSON towed the EAGLE into Sandusky today.

March 9. EAGLE came out late this P.M. Thick fog this P.M. and evening. Lit up for the EAGLE.

June 1. U.S. Lt. House Tender HAZE passed into Sandusky at 9 A.M. Came to off this station at 4 P.M. and cleared at 6 P.M. bound up. Commander Gridley, Captain Baxter and Engineer came ashore. Made inspection and left supplies.

July 26. Lighthouse Keeper H.A. Lyman of Cedar Point came to this station this A.M.

February 23, 1888. The Steamer AMERICAN EAGLE which has been layed up the past 30 days for repairs to her boiler and machinery, came out today, passed this station at 5:00 P.M. up the Lake. The light at the station was relit today.

February 13, 1889. Discontinued the light this A.M. as the EAGLE will not be out again for a few days.

March 2. Relit the light again tonight after having been out 17 nights. The AMERICAN EAGLE has been hard off this station this P.M. and evening working her way through the ice from Put-In-Bay to Sandusky. She could not be seen from this station on acct. of fog.

March 3. The AMERICAN EAGLE was again seen this A.M. off Cedar Point shoreline. Has been laid up in the ice all night.

June 11. Admiral Harmony, Chairman of the Lighthouse Board and Capt. Chas. V. Gridley inspected that station. Captain Baxter delivered the annual supplies.

August 15. The stmr. B.F. FERRIS which has run on the Sandusky, Marblehead and Catawba Island route the past 20 years left for New Baltimore last night to which place she has been sold.

August 17. The new sidewheeler Stmr. A. WHERLE, JR. came out on her first trip today.

August 20, 1891. 18 years ago today I took charge of this station.

December 27. No vessel having been sighted during the past week, the light at this station was discontinued this morning.

December 29. At 6:30 tonight I heard the sound of a whistle on the Lake. Therefore the light at this station was relit at that time.

(In 1892 and 1893 Keeper McGee made frequent trips to the dentist in Sandusky and to the doctor to have his throat treated. In October, 1893 he went to the World's Fair in Chicago. Much of the log from here on was written by his wife and his daughters.)

May 1, 1894. The Keeper has been confined to the dwelling by sickness since March 23rd and today was able to be out of doors a short time. During the past month the keeper has had a man employed to do the painting, clean the lamps–lens and at his own expense. His daughter Mattie has had entire charge of the lighthouse.

August 29. The keeper started for Cincinnati at 6 A.M. to take a physical examination.

August 30. U.S.S. SWANSEA came to off the station this P.M. Lieut. Col. Jared A. Smith, U.S. LH. Engineer came ashore and inspected this station.

August 31. The Keeper returned from Cincinnati this morning at 11:00 A.M.

October 11. George H. McGee, Keeper of this Station, left this morning at 10 A.M. on Str. R. B. HAYES for the South on account of ill health.

December 28. Large floe of ice came from up the Lake today. Small schooner passed this Station at 4:15 P.M. and became fast in the ice near Cedar Point.

December 29. Str. AMERICAN EAGLE towed the same schooner. MAPLE LEAF, from Cedar Point, passed this Point at 3:30 and up the Lake.

June 2, 1895 The Keeper returned to this Station 15 2:00 P.M. after an absence of 8 months–less 7 days–in the Southern states for the benefit of his health. The following route was taken. To Sandusky–Cincinnati–St. Louis–Mississippi River–New Orleans–Gulf of Mexico–Tampa–DeLand–Titusville–Cape Canaveral–Enterprise–St. Johns River–Jacksonville–Savannah–Atlantic Ocean–Baltimore–Washington–Pittsburgh–Cleveland–Sandusky–then to Marblehead Light Station, his health has been benefited by the trip, although he passed through a very severe winter in Florida.

June 7. Rose, the cow, died at noon today.

June 12. Set the wooden cistern up under the walnut tree.

September 16. During the past week the tower has been whitewashed, it required 4 bu. lime, 25# salt, almost 5 bbl. Whitewash, one man in boatwains chair 31 3/4 hours, a tender 31 3/4 hours who whitewashed from the ground and ladder 10 1/2 hours of the 31 3/4 the balance of the time was consumed in mixing whitewash and waiting on the man aloft.

April 20, 1896. Warm and bright in the fore-noon but afternoon the wind blew perfectly terrible and the rain came down in torrents.

May 3. Papa out on the porch for three hours for a sun bath.

June 30. The Keeper George McGee died at this station June 17, 1896, age 45 years.

July 8. Mrs. Johanna McGee has this day been appointed keeper of this station.

November 3. Wm. McKinley was elected President. Marblehead went 19 Rep. majority something never known before.

November 11. The carpenters finished wood shed.

November 12. The carpenters commenced work on the barn.

November 13. This P.M. one of the carpenters, W. Carrel, sprained his back while moving old barn and had to quit work for more than a week.

November 20. Stmr. HAZE passed down to take up buoys in Sandusky Bay. Mattie went to W.N. Payne's to get a barrel of cider.

July 13, 1897. Three water spouts were seen on the lake today.

July 17. Two more have been sighted, a meteorological phenomenon, is the first witnessed here.

August 18. Col. J.A. Smith, wife and son and Major Blunt, wife, daughter and son, and Blunt inspected this station to see about work to be done on the tower.

August 20. J.P. Bumpus and J. Case arrived from Sandusky this A.M. to repair tower.

August 27. Charlie Cooper and Thomas Fowler commenced cutting stone for tower windows. Sherm Green finished hauling 1 car of brick for tower at $1.00 per thousand.

September 2. Jesse P. Bumpus is getting along nicely with the Lt. H. Tower. The following men are at work for U. Sam. Gerald Hazen, Albion, Wm. Schmidt, Marblehead, J.L. Case, Vermilion, Joe Horkie, Henry Geisman, Dewey Wolcott, Lakeside, John Rothacker, Fremont.

September 27. U.S.Lt.H. Tender HAZE passed down this 3 P.M. Re'cd from the Engineer's office, Lighthouse Depot, Tompkinsville, Staten Island, N.Y. three lamps measurements incl. Height from base to focus 15 3/16 in. Diameter of ring 7 3/8 in. and the old lamps are to be returned. Inspected Oct. 4, 1897.

July 13, 1898. Millions of flys in the lantern this A.M. Do not know how they got in unless through the crack of the door. Cleaned lenses and lantern window.

November 4. Mr. Fred Barker and Ed Gamble arrived here this A.M. from Put-In-Bay to put up a water hoist on the top of the tower for hoisting up water, to put up carriage house, new stairs into the cellar, and other minor repairs.

November 20. All went to church this A.M. Wind NE. Mrs. Joseph Gibeaut (Green Island lighthouse keeper's wife) died this evening at Green Springs, 0.

April 13, 1899. Clara and myself went to Sandusky for Alice's graduation.

April 23. Wind NE cold. Alice took teachers examination at Oak Harbor.

November 3. Old Doll broke her leg, was shot.

November 25. Mr. Gamble and Nailor commenced whitewashing Tower.

November 27. Put a cement floor in Tower and two wooden doors to take place of iron doors, also screens for two of the Tower windows.

December 6. Seven cases of Small Pox at Lakeside. All public places have been ordered closed by the Board of Health.

May 28, 1900. Inspected May 28, 1900. Station in very good order. (signed) Franklin Harford, Comdr. U.S.N., L.H. inspector.

September 4. Lampest finished work on lens today and the keeper left for Adrian, Mich., with her daughter Hannah to enter the Academy, left the light station in charge of daughter, Alice. SW and very warm.

October 4. Put up tomatoes.

October 10. Canned peaches, pickled peaches and cucumbers.

October 12. Cleaned coal shed and took screens out of windows.

October 14. Pickled tomatoes, washed windows and picked apples.

October 17. Picked apples. U.S. Tender HAZE passed into Sandusky Bay this 3:15 P.M. Cleaned cistern.

December 3. SW Heavy dew. Took off deck and tore out ceiling of watchroom.

December 20. The work on the Tower was finished today until further notice, and the fixed white light of the fourth order is established and light again is exhibited. Sent reports.

May 29, 1901. F. and Hesper fought. Hep. had his jaw split, shot and buried him. Whitewashed chicken coop and washed lantern windows.

July 14. John went for sub for Si Sauvey at the L.S. Station.

August 15. Returned from Gallion today on the Str. EAGLE. Str. WASHINGTON came to off this station this 12:30. Major Symons inspected Station, ordered the Keeper to have a Terra Cotta cap put on the kitchen chimney, also to have the dwelling painted as soon as possible.

September 7. NE fresh breeze. President McKinley shot at Buffalo, Friday 4:30 P.M. Sept. 6, 1901 by Leon Czolgsz, not fatally wounded.

September 10. SE gale. President's condition much improved, and is believed will recover.

April 10, 1902. Str. ARROW made her first trip of the season.

April 14. NW, light rain. Str. FRANK E. KIRBY made her first trip of the season.

April 26. NW gale. A fearful storm is raging. The Schr. BARKLOW from Marine City foundered half mile from Put-In-Bay. Capt. Pardy, wife and son drowned. The body of Mrs. Pardy washed ashore at Put-In-Bay. Dick Bunk, a sailor, survived and taken to Sandusky on tug JOHN MONK.

August 10. The keeper called on Mr. O. Mason, Keeper of the South Bass light 12 m to 4 P.M.

August 12. Mr. Barker and Gamble arrived from South Bass. Put screens on ventilator in Tower.

August 26. Mrs. Pope called today. Lighthouse Keeper's wife from Port Clinton.

October 1. Alice started to work for Mr. Braithwaite.

January 29, 1903. Finished putting in a Third Order lends and apparatus, the old 4th Order lens was shipped to Buffalo by the lampest Mr. W.C. Helbig.

March 16. Mr. Chas. A. Hunter, Asst. Keeper of Thirty Mile Point Lt. Station, reported at this station for duty to succeed Mrs. J. H. McGee as keeper.

March 17. Commenced packing up today.

March 19. Finished storing my household goods in Milo Clemon's house.

March 23. Mr. Hunter's household goods arrived today.

(The remaining log notations were made by the new keeper, Charles Hunter.)

April 2. Clinton Egelton reported for duty as Ass't. Keeper, from Toledo, Ohio.

April 4. Mr. Egelton's household goods arrived. Cleaned barn. Mrs. Egelton arrived.

April 6. Found body of mail carrier at Lakeside with one criper and a skate on.

April 25. Lantern large glass cracked way across.

May 5. Str. WARRINGTON stopped and took away bricks, timbers, 4th lens glass and 1 box chimney holders.

May 9. Painting inside of lantern white.

May 11. Painting inside of Tower.

May 12. Painting stairs in Tower.

May 17. Started on new Journal.

5

Vows and Visitors

Lighthouses, in addition to their usefulness as beacons for mariners, are romantic places. Take, for example, the Minot's Ledge Lighthouse perched on a treacherous rock ledge just off Cohasset, Massachusetts, and known as the "I Love You" lighthouse because of its unique signal: one flash, four flashes, and then three flashes at 45 second intervals. A similar romantic attachment holds for the Marblehead Lighthouse where, in addition to hundreds of people who visit it in every season of the year to photograph, to sketch and paint, to climb, or only to gaze at it, some come to get married on the spacious green lawn, on the solid stone beach, or at the top of the tower with its breathtaking view.

An early wedding at the lighthouse took place on January 1, 1856 when Alvira, daughter of the lighthouse keeper, Jared Keyes, and his wife, Arvilla Knapp Wolcott, married William Alexander Clemons, son of

Alexander Clemons and his wife, Alma Angeline Hollister. The bride was the granddaughter of Benajah Wolcott, first keeper of the Marblehead Lighthouse.

Since that time other weddings have taken place, though not in the keeper's house as William and Alvira's was but in the lighthouse itself and on the surrounding grounds. Although there is no record of the ceremonies that have been performed over the years, they are still going on today.

Kay Dziak, the mayor of Marblehead since January, 1988, who is licensed to perform weddings, has officiated at numerous ceremonies for people from all over Ohio who have nostalgic and sentimental feelings about the venerable lighthouse. Some are second marriages, some are formal weddings with long dresses and tuxedos, and some have been performed in chilly weather or in the rain. Since she does not like heights, she has had to get used to performing the ceremony at the top of the tower. One wedding at which she officiated occurred the same day the lighthouse was open to visitors; during the ceremony, the tower was closed off to tourists lined up to climb the lighthouse, and, as the bridal party emerged, they applauded.

Richard and Janet Gaudern Fallat, who grew up on the shores of Lake Erie, have strong attachments to this lighthouse. Richard, formerly of Cleveland, and Janet, whose parents, Tom and Rita Gaudern, were pioneers in the charter boat business in Port Clinton, were married at the lighthouse on June 30, 1979. Two and a half days before the wedding, there had been a nor'easter, usually a severe three-day storm: it rained and blew a gale. At 11:00 o'clock on Saturday morning, the sun shone for the first time in days, and the ceremony went on as planned.

Al and Janett St. Clair decided to get married at the lighthouse because it seemed appropriate. Since Al's family had been commercial fishermen and marsh

Figure 5-1. *Janice Reynolds and Bill Gstalder were married on September 14, 1985, at the base of the lighthouse. Both love the water; Janice grew up in Port Clinton and Bill spent all of his early summers camping at Bay Point. The September day was perfect: sunny, warm, just a little breeze, and the foliage was starting to turn color. A day to remember.* Photo courtesy of the Gstalders.

managers at the Toussaint and Cedar Point marshes for generations, both have loved Marblehead and the lighthouse. They were married at the top on April 13, 1991—a cloudy and overcast day. Despite a fear of heights, the best man got through the ceremony all right, but the minister had to pry his hands off the struts to hand him the ring.

The renewal of wedding vows also take place at the lighthouse. Ethel May and Donald Inman of Marblehead chose November 23, 1988 as the date for such a ceremony at the top. The Reverend Janine Dress conducted the ceremony, and a member of the U.S. Coast Guard, who opened the lighthouse, served as a witness.

Robert Reiger, U.S. Coast Guard Auxillary official in charge of arranging tours, had a request for a tour to the top. When he asked how many would be on the tour, an embarrassed young man said, "Well, um, er, just two of us. You see, I want to propose to my girlfriend at the top of the lighthouse." The request was granted; he proposed and she accepted.

"Cap" Hunter, keeper of the lighthouse, welcomed visitors for many years (including the writer of this book) but after his retirement in 1933 the practice was discontinued. Then, in 1985, interest in lighthouse tours was rekindled when James Kriner, operations officer with the U.S. Coast Guard, coordinated the efforts of the Peninsula Chamber of Commerce, village council members, Danbury Township trustees, and the Marblehead Coast Guard in organizing tours. The first tour, held in September, 1985, proved so successful that between 2,000 and 3,000 people had to be turned away; cars, trucks, and vans were lined up for hours while groups of ten people spent five to ten minutes touring the lighthouse while others waited in line for a chance to see the inside of the historic structure.

Tours are conducted on the second Saturday of June, July, August, and September, with the U.S. Coast Guard Auxiliary in charge. Visitors come not only from Ohio and other states but from many foreign countries. In 1994, 2,278 persons toured the lighthouse and the U.S. Coast Guard Station in Marblehead. Visitors

Figure 5-2. *On four Saturdays during the summer months, visitors to the lighthouse come from everywhere to climb the 87 steps to the top. They are rewarded with a spectacular view of Lake Erie, the islands, Cedar Point, and the Marblehead Peninsula. They also come to marvel at the historic beacon which has been guiding vessels without interruption since 1822. Truly, this is Lake Erie's eternal flame. Author's photo.*

are also directed to the family home of the first keeper of the lighthouse, Benajah Wolcott, on Bayshore Road. The home, which is one of the oldest structures in Northwestern Ohio, is being restored and preserved by the Ottawa County Historical Society. Nearby is the Wolcott family cemetery as well as the site of the initial skirmish of the War of 1812.

Bibliography

Books

Adamson, Hans Christian. *Keepers of the Lights*. New York: Greenberg: 1955.

Commemorative Biographical Record of the Counties of Sandusky and Ottawa, Ohio. Chicago: J.H. Beers and Company, 1986.

Frohman, Charles E. *Sandusky's Yesterdays*. Columbus, Ohio: Ohio Historical Society, 1968.

Hatcher, Harlan. *Lake Erie*. Indianapolis, New York: Bobbs-Merrill Co.. 1945.

Havighurst, Walter. *The Long Ships Passing, The Story of the Great Lakes*. New York: The Macmillan Company, 1961.

Holland, Francis Ross, Jr. *Great American Lighthouses*. Washington D.C.: The Preservation Press, 1989.

Holland, Francis Ross, Jr. *America's Lighthouses, An Illustrated History*. Mineola, New York: Dover Publications, Inc.., 1988.

Majdalany, Fred. *The Eddystone Light*. Boston: Houghton Mifflin Company, 1960.

Moseley, Edwin Lincoln. *Lake Erie Floods, Lake Levels, Northeast Storms: The Formation of Sandusky Bay and Cedar Point.* Columbus, Ohio: The Ohio Historical Society, 1973.

O'Brien, T. Michael. *Guardians of the Eighth Sea: A History of the U.S. Coast Guard on the Great Lakes: The Ninth Coast Guard District.*

Shepard, Birse. *Lore of the Wreckers.* Boston: Beacon Press, 1961.

Tiessen. Ronald. *A Bicycle Guide to Pelee Island* (Second Edition). Pelee Island, Ontario, Canada, Pelee Island Heritage Center, 1992.

Van, Benschoten. *William Henry. Concerning the Van Benschoten or Van Bunschoten Family in America.* West Park on Hudson, New York, 1907.

Wendt, Gordon. *In The Wake of The Walk-In-The-Water: The Marine History of Sandusky, Ohio.* Sandusky, Ohio: Commercial Printing Co., 1984.

Williams, W.W. *History of the Firelands, Comprising Huron and Erie Counties, with Illustrations and Biographical Sketches of Some of the Prominent Men and Pioneers.* Cleveland: Leader Printing Company, 1879.

Periodicals

Agard, A.H. "Historical Sketches of Danbury Township." *The Firelands Pioneer.* June, 1870.

Kelly, Malcolm. "Some Bits of Local History." *The Firelands Pioneer.* N.S. Vol. XXI1, January, 1921.

Proceedings, Quarterly Meeting of the Firelands Historical Society. "Hours With the Pioneers: Old Times On The Firelands." *The Firelands Pioneer,* June, 1868.

Wolcott, Merlin. "Marblehead Lighthouse." *Inland Seas,* Vol. 10, No. 4, Winter, 1954.

Public Documents

Census Reports, 1870. Ottawa County Genealogical Society. Ida Rupp Public Library, Port Clinton, Ohio.

Common Pleas Court. Probate Division, Huron County, Ohio. Record of Marriages, April 24, 1822.

"Debates and Proceedings of the Congress of the United States, Fifteenth Congress, Second Session Comprising the Period from

Nov. 16. 1818 to March 3, 1819, Inclusive." History of Congress, March, 1819, pp. 1425 and 1426.

Library of Congress, Geography and Map Division, Washington, D.C.

National Archives and Records Administration, Records of the United States Coast Guard, Record Group 26. Records of the Bureau of Lighthouses and Its Predecessors, 1789-1939.

Revolutionary War Records Section. Department of the Interior, Bureau of Pensions, Washington D.C., October 9, 1914.

Programs, Pamphlets, Manuscripts, Clippings

Great Lakes Historical Society. Vermilion, Ohio. Clipping file.

Hesselbart, May. "Our Predecessor – The American Indian." Unpublished manuscript, Ottawa County Historical Museum, 1960.

Journal of the Marblenead Lighthouse Station, 1872 to 1903. MMS998. Center for Archival Collections, Bowling Green State University, Bowling Green, Ohio.

Merlin Wolcott Papers. Unpublished manuscript collection. MS694. Center for Archival Collections. Bowling Green State University. Bowling Green, Ohio.

Moon, Paul. '"Benajah Wolcott. 1762-1832." Brochure given to tourists visiting the Keeper's House. The Ottawa County Historical Society.

"Peninsula Chamber of Commerce." Fact sheet on the Marblehead Lighthouse given to visitors at the Lighthouse.

Schultz, Alice Haas. *Marblehead Lifesaving Station Collection*. MS278. Center for Archival Collections, Bowling Green State University, Bowling Green, Ohio.

Wonnell, Marie. "The History of the Marblehead Lighthouse." Unpublished manuscript, pOG2924. Center for Archival Collections, Bowling Green State University, Bowling Green, Ohio.

Index

D

E

F

G

H

I

J

K

L

M

N

O

P

R

S

T

U

V

W